Blueprints 1

Blueprints 1

COMPOSITION SKILLS FOR ACADEMIC WRITING

Keith S. Folse
University of Central Florida

M. Kathleen Mahnke
Saint Michael's College

Elena Vestri Solomon
Teacher Trainer, UzTEA Uzbekistan

Lorraine Williams
Saint Michael's College

Houghton Mifflin Company
Boston • New York

Editor in Chief: *Patricia A. Coryell*
Director of ESL Publishing: *Susan Maguire*
Senior Development Editor: *Kathleen Sands Boehmer*
Editorial Assistant: *Mira Bharin*
Senior Project Editor: *Kathryn Dinovo*
Cover Design Manager: *Diana Coe*
Senior Manufacturing Coordinator: *Jane Spelman*
Marketing Manager: *Annamarie Rice*
Marketing Assistant: *Sophie Xie*

Cover image: © Ryan McVay / Getty Images / PhotoDisc

Photo Credits: **p. 1:** © Eric Kamp/Index Stock Imagery. **p. 8:** © Tony Arruza/CORBIS. **p. 10:** © Richard T. Nowitz/CORBIS. **p. 26 (top left):** © Richard T. Nowitz/CORBIS. **p. 26 (top right):** © Kevin R. Morris/CORBIS. **p. 26 (bottom left):** © Danny Lehman/ CORBIS. **p. 26 (bottom right):** © Scott T. Smith/CORBIS. **p. 40:** © Lonnie Duka/Index Stock Imagery. **p. 65:** © Eric Kamp/Index Stock Imagery. **p. 92:** © Ryan McVay/Getty Images. **p. 96:** © Reuters NewsMedia Inc./CORBIS. **p. 120:** © Izzy Schwartz/Getty Images. **p. 149:** © Ryan McVay/Getty Images.

college.hmco.com

Printed in the U.S.A.

Library of Congress Control Number: 2001131496

ISBN: 0-618-14409-9

6 7 8 9-HS-06 05

CONTENTS

Unit 1
THE PARAGRAPH   1

Unit 5
COMPARISON/CONTRAST
PARAGRAPHS   120

BLUEPRINTS 1 SKILLS CHART

Unit	Blueprint	Transition Expressions	Writing from Sources: Paraphrasing, Summarizing, and Synthesizing
1 The Paragraph	What Is a Paragraph? Sources: Reading and Analyzing Sample Paragraphs	*in addition (to),* *though,* *although,* *later*	Definitions of and practice with paraphrasing, summarizing, and synthesizing
2 Descriptive Paragraphs	What Is a Descriptive Paragraph? Sources: Reading and Analyzing Sample Paragraphs	*when,* *while,* *as,* *after*	More practice with paraphrasing, summarizing, and synthesizing
3 Process Paragraphs	What Is a Process Paragraph? Sources: Reading and Analyzing Sample Paragraphs	*first,* *next,* *then,* *finally*	More practice with paraphrasing, summarizing, and synthesizing
4 Definition Paragraphs	What Is a Definition Paragraph? Sources: Reading and Analyzing Sample Paragraphs	*this (+ noun),* *according to,* *in fact*	More practice with paraphrasing, summarizing, and synthesizing
5 Comparison/ Contrast Paragraphs	What Is a Comparison/Contrast Paragraph? Sources: Reading and Analyzing Sample Paragraphs	*like,* *the same . . . as,* *in contrast,* *whereas*	More practice with paraphrasing, summarizing, and synthesizing
6 Introducing the Essay	What Is an Essay? From Paragraph to Essay: An Example	*for example,* *for instance,* *one . . . ,* *another . . . ,* *such as*	Working with essay outlines

BLUEPRINTS 1 SKILLS CHART

Prewriting	Planning	Process	Grammar Focus
Brainstorming	Lists and Outlining	· First draft · partner feedback · second draft · editing · final draft	Singular and plural forms of count nouns
Freewriting	Sequencing ideas with a flowchart	· First draft · partner feedback · second draft · editing · final draft	Using prepositions of location, direction, and time
Interest questionnaire, Subject agreement	Chronological steps	· First draft · partner feedback · second draft · editing · final draft	Subject agreement
List of general nouns and adjective clauses process	Important details	· First draft · partner feedback · second draft · editing · final draft	Practice correct use of articles *a, an, the*
Answer open-ended questions to generate ideas	Similarities and differences in a chart	· First draft · partner feedback · second draft · editing · final draft	Practice using *more, most, -er, -est, as . . . as; the same . . . as*
Brainstorming	Write thesis, topic sentences, and supporting details in an outline	· First draft · partner feedback · second draft · editing · final draft	Verb tense review

BLUEPRINTS 1 SKILLS CHART

Unit	Sentence Check	Mechanics	Additional Writing Assignments From the Academic Disciplines
1 The Paragraph	Practice writing complete sentences that always include a verb	Use commas with certain transition words	– Science – Computers – Business – Architecture
2 Descriptive Paragraphs	Sentence parts, including subject, verb, object, adjective, and prepositional phrase	Use commas with prepositional phrases	– Business – Culture – Science – Media studies – Health care
3 Process Paragraphs	Identify compound sentences patterns with *and, but, so, or*	Learn correct paragraph title format	– Technology – Science – Sociology – Practical
4 Definition Paragraphs	Identify adjective clauses (*who, that, which, Ø*)	Learn correct punctuation with restrictive and nonrestrictive adjective clauses	– Culture/anthropology – Chemistry – Health care – U.S. history – Architecture – Practical
5 Comparison/ Contrast Paragraphs	Identify and practice writing use dependent noun clauses	Capitalization of titles review	– Business – Culture – Media studies – Health care
6 Introducing the Essay	Adverb clauses	Format of an essay	– Technology – Science – The arts – Management – Practical

WELCOME TO BLUEPRINTS!

Blueprints: Composition Skills for Academic Writing, First Edition is a two-volume writing series for students of English as a second language. *Blueprints 1* is designed for intermediate-level students. *Blueprints 2* is designed for students at the high-intermediate and advanced levels. Both books are aimed at preparing students for success in academic writing. *Blueprints 1* focuses primarily on the paragraph, with a final unit devoted to the essay. *Blueprints 2* moves students from the paragraph to the essay in its first unit and focuses on the essay from that point on. Each *Blueprints* text features direct instruction in academic composition skills, short reading passages that serve as springboards for writing tasks, presentations of key ESL grammar points, a large number of practice exercises, and a variety of real writing assignments.

TO THE TEACHER

Series Approach

Recent research in ESL writing instruction points to the inextricable link between the two skills of reading and writing. The *Blueprints* series builds on this connection by using reading to support the instruction of writing. For example, students using *Blueprints* practice reading for main ideas, details, and so forth, before practicing these features in their writing. In addition, in both *Blueprints 1* and *Blueprints 2*, students read and analyze numerous "blueprint" model paragraphs and essays that exemplify the rhetorical modes and other techniques of writing that they are learning. Connections between reading and writing are exploited throughout both texts to the maximum benefit of students.

Over the past several years, research and practice in the teaching of ESL writing have established both the writing process and the written product as important instructional focuses. With this in mind, another key component of the *Blueprints* approach is the incorporation of writing process/product practice. In each unit, a writing topic is assigned and students follow a series of process steps, from prewriting through peer- and teacher-review of various drafts to a final, finished product. This portion of each unit incorporates the most current philosophies regarding the importance of the writing process, including audience response and feedback, to the creation of a final written product.

Both volumes 1 and 2 of *Blueprints* provide instruction in the rhetorical modes that make up the bulk of academic writing across the disciplines. Additionally, the texts help students work on topic and thesis statements, introductions, body sentences and paragraphs, and conclusions.

Blueprints 1

A unique feature of the *Blueprints* series is the addition of three important, yet often neglected, aspects of academic writing: **paraphrasing, summarizing,** and **synthesizing** information from more than one source. Other composition topics that are treated include reaction paper writing as well as special attention to techniques for assuring coherence and unity in writing. In particular, the practices involving paraphrasing, summarizing, and synthesizing represent an innovative way for learners to hone their abilities with these extremely important composition skills.

Another important feature of the *Blueprints* series approach is its attention to grammar instruction and practice. Both ESL teachers and ESL students recognize that grammar surfaces as a particularly challenging element of second-language writing. With this in mind, grammar points that are particularly useful to writers at the intermediate and advanced levels are explained, exemplified in the model readings, and practiced in each unit of both *Blueprints* books.

About the Books

Each *Blueprints* text begins with an introductory unit. In *Blueprints 1*, this unit presents the paragraph as well as the skills of paraphrasing, summarizing, and synthesizing. In its first unit, *Blueprints 2* introduces the essay, various techniques for writing introductions and conclusions, and the concepts of unity and coherence. The remaining units in each book are organized around rhetorical modes, with special attention given to other selected aspects of academic writing. (See individual tables of contents for details.)

Each unit in the *Blueprints* texts is divided into two parts. Part A is the instructional portion. Part B leads the student through the steps of the writing process as it applies to the rhetorical mode introduced in the unit. Each part begins with a clearly stated list of objectives so that teachers and students alike can determine the relevance of these objectives to real student needs.

TO THE STUDENT

Without a doubt, good writing requires many skills. Good writing requires your ability to use words and sentences correctly, and very good writing requires the ability to organize these words and sentences into paragraphs and essays that readers can understand well. Good writing means mastery of basic punctuation, capitalization, and spelling rules. In addition, good writing includes a solid grasp of English sentence structure, or grammar, to express ideas in writing that is accurate and appropriate.

Good writing in an academic setting often requires you to take information from one or more sources to produce a piece of writing that satisfies a certain writing task. Common examples of these academic writing tasks include summarizing a story, reacting to a piece of writing, and combining information into a new paragraph or essay.

Blueprints prepares you to be a good academic writer. One of the primary goals of the *Blueprints* books is to help you move beyond writing simple paragraphs and essays that are based on general or personal information to writing paragraphs and essays that are based on academic-level readings. The tasks in these books mirror what you will have to do in your college-level courses.

The following chart lists some special features of the *Blueprints* texts and their benefits to you.

FEATURE	BENEFIT
Blueprint readings exemplifying writing	The readings provide examples of good writing.
Two readings on similar/same topics	The readings provide opportunities to develop vocabulary fluency and understanding on a single topic.
Grammar instruction and practice	The grammar instruction and practice help student writers master grammar in their writing.
Paraphrasing, summarizing, and synthesizing practice	These three specific skills may be the best help students will ever find for composition.
Academic writing assignments at the end of each unit	Student writing can actually reflect their learning goals.

PREFACE TO BLUEPRINTS 1

Text Organization

Blueprints 1 is divided into six units. Unit 1 introduces the elements of a good paragraph. Units 2 through 5 provide practice in four different kinds of paragraphs. Unit 6 introduces the basics of a good essay.

This book is organized with a writing or rhetorical mode at the paragraph level as the primary vehicle of practicing organized composition. Unit 2 practices descriptive paragraphs, perhaps the simplest of the various kinds of paragraphs. Unit 3 focuses on process paragraphs. Unit 4 features definition paragraphs. Unit 5 provides practice in comparison/contrast paragraphs. These four rhetorical modes were chosen because surveys of college and university programs cited them as those most often taught in freshman writing programs.

At the back of the book is an appendix containing the partner feedback forms needed for the activities in *Blueprints 1*. Instead of generic checklists for student writing, the peer review sheets in this book have been specifically designed for the particular writing assignment in that unit.

Contents of a Unit

Part A

Composition Lesson

Each unit begins with the core material for the unit, consisting of a presentation of the rhetorical mode for that unit. This presentation is followed by a series of short exercises that provide step-by-step practice with the writing lesson in the unit.

Readings

Because of the important link between reading and writing, each unit (except unit 6) contains two short reading passages (150–250 words) that students work with before they attempt any evaluation of a simple essay. Each reading passage is preceded by a brief set of questions that helps to activate the schema necessary for reading comprehension. Each reading contains glossed key vocabulary terms as well as questions that require students to analyze not only the content of the passage, but also various composition components that are featured in the reading passage. The focus on vocabulary is extremely important because a more solid grasp of lexical items will help students to move from basic writing to more advanced writing. Likewise, the focus on composition components provides not only focused instruction but also sufficient guided practice.

Because students are required to work with both of the readings in each unit to produce a written assignment, the two reading passages deal with the same or similar topics. This use of a theme-based approach to reading and writing is useful for many learners and teachers in that it helps learners develop a common content base in addition to a common vocabulary base for discussing and writing about that particular topic.

Paraphrasing, Summarizing, and Synthesizing

The main focus of *Blueprints 1* is academic writing, primarily at the paragraph level. Students in an academic preparation program need to go beyond writing about their experiences in narrative form. These students need to be able to read various pieces of information on a topic, decide which information is relevant to their writing assignment needs, put the information in their own words, and then compile this in a fluent, organized written work. To accomplish this goal, students must be able to paraphrase, summarize, and synthesize. To this end, *Blueprints 1* contains specific instruction and exercises for each of these three critical skills.

Paraphrasing

Each unit (except Unit 6) contains two exercises that practice paraphrasing. In the first exercise, students read an original sentence from Reading 1 and then must choose which of three sentences is the best paraphrase for the original sentence. This is followed by an original sentence from Reading 2 and the same multiple-choice question.

In the second exercise, students must read another key sentence from Reading 1 and select which of three sentences offers the best paraphrase. This is followed by an original sentence from Reading 2, and students must write original paraphrases of the sentence.

Thus, the two exercises practice not only passive recognition of correct paraphrases but also active production of accurate paraphrases.

Summarizing

Each unit (except Unit 6) contains a summarizing activity in which students are asked to summarize a particular reading passage (i.e., one of the two reading passages in the unit). Reminder notes on the use of a topic sentence and organization as well as guidelines on the length of the student summary are provided. On the basis of the length of the original passage, students are told not to exceed a certain number of words in their summary.

The design of this summarizing activity has several advantages. First, by the time the students reach this activity, they have already become very familiar with the content of the reading passage, including grammatical structures, vocabulary items, punctuation hints, the overall meaning of the passage, and the specific meaning of individual sentences. Instructors can be assured that students know the content of each passage well enough to explain it in their own words. Second, all of the students are able to work with the same passage, which means that this activity can be done by the whole class and can be checked in class either on the board or as a pair work or group work activity. Finally, the use of the same passage for the whole class allows for more concentration on actual writing. Rather than having all of the students working with individual topics, the use of a single reading passage that has been carefully analyzed by the students removes the possibility that the language of the passage will be a hindrance in writing a summary. Students can think more about the content and language of what they will write instead of the content and language of what they have read.

Synthesizing

Students in an academic course must be able to read different sources, choose what is important on the basis of the assignment, and then write an accurate paragraph or essay that synthesizes the pertinent information from the sources in the students' own words. To practice this skill, *Blueprints 1* features a synthesizing activity in every unit (except Unit 6). In this activity, students are presented with a hypothetical question from an academic course. The question requires the students to use the information from the two reading passages. Again, general guidelines regarding length of the synthesized paragraph are provided in the directions.

For example, in Unit 4 ("Definition Paragraphs"), Reading 1 defines HIV, and Reading 2 defines AIDS. The question that prompts students to write a synthesized paragraph is on a hypothetical health exam. The question prompt reads:

> Many people confuse HIV and AIDS, but these two terms actually refer to separate things. On the basis of what you have learned about HIV and AIDS, write a paragraph defining them. In your discussion, include differences in symptoms and infection rates.

Sometimes the required information is in only one of the reading passages, and the students' main task is paraphrasing the information from that reading. At other times, the information is stated in both readings. In this case, students must determine whether the information is stated equally well in both readings or whether it is better stated in one of the readings. In both of these cases, students must decide which information to select for inclusion in the final writing product as well as how to paraphrase the material and then interweave it with other information.

Part B

Writing Assignment

In each unit, students are given a specific writing assignment that is based on the rhetorical mode presented in that unit. In Unit 4, for example, students write an original definition paragraph. By having all the students work on the same assignment, the writing instructor has an opportunity to teach the whole group. At any point during the writing process, the teacher and class can address areas of concern.

Prewriting

Each unit presents some type of prewriting activity. This particular activity varies from unit to unit. (See chart on p. xi.)

First Draft

As students write their first draft, a special checklist based on the rhetorical mode is provided to help them at this point.

Partner Feedback

Working with classmates is a valuable process for many reasons. Group work is required in many academic classes, so practice with a familiar and sympathetic ESL audience is helpful. Group work also allows students to exchange ideas about a given topic. Finally, group work can be valuable because other student readers tend to be more critical than the writer and therefore more likely to find errors than self-editing could.

Appendix 5 at the back of the book contains special forms for partner feedback. Each form has been designed to take into account the rhetorical mode being practiced, the type of writing prompt, and the kinds of grammar issues usually present in this rhetorical mode.

Second Draft

At this point, another checklist is provided. This checklist covers a few of the questions on the first checklist but also has many new questions about the contents of this second draft.

Editing: Grammar and Mechanics

Because grammar is such an integral part of any good writing, there are two kinds of grammar presentations in each unit: discrete grammar and sentence-level grammar. The points practiced in these two categories vary from unit to unit. In addition, a mechanics feature is presented in each unit. These vary from unit to unit. An example of one of the mechanics features is the use of commas.

Final Draft

At this point, students are asked to review their final draft to check their language use, mechanics, and writing conventions.

Additional Writing Assignments from the Academic Disciplines

A unique feature of this book is a chart appearing at the end of every unit. This chart features a list of four to six academic areas with a writing prompt for a topic in each one. The writing prompts lend themselves well to the rhetorical mode being presented and practiced in that particular unit.

Appendixes

In addition to the appendix for Partner Feedback Forms, *Blueprints 1* provides an appendix on documenting sources and three appendixes on common grammatical and punctuation problems.

Instructor's Notes and Extra Exercises

Helpful notes for instructors using *Blueprints 1*, as well as extra exercises for students, are also available at www.hmco.com/college.

ACKNOWLEDGMENTS

This book and its companion text *Blueprints II* are the result of a tremendous amount of work, research, and discussion as well as L2 teaching experience and L2 learning experience on effective ways to improve second language writing. We would like to thank those educators and learners who helped us arrive at our current understanding of L2 writing by sharing their insights, teaching ideas, and learning hints.

The four of us offer a very special word of thanks to our editors at Houghton Mifflin, who have been so great throughout the development of the *Blueprints* books. Huge thanks go to Susan Maguire, who has been a constant source of guidance and inspiration from the very inception of this series. Likewise, we are tremendously indebted to Kathy Sands Boehmer, who provided just the right amounts of positive feedback and gentle nudging throughout the completion of this project. In addition, we are forever grateful to our developmental editor, Kathleen Smith, whose careful editing and diligent work have played an integral role in the creation of this final product.

We would also like to thank the following reviewers who offered ideas and suggestions that shaped our revisions: Leslie Biaggi, Miami Dade Community College; Sharon Bode, University of Pennsylvania; Jane Curtis, Roosevelt University; Linda Forse, University of Texas, Brownsville; Tamar Goldmann, Orange Coast Community College; Zeljana Grubisic, University of Maryland at Baltimore County; Darryl Kinney, Los Angeles City College; Manuel Muñoz; Sally Patterson, Mt. San Antonio College; John Stasinopoulos, College of DuPage.

Keith S. Folse
M. Kathleen Mahnke
Elena Vestri Solomon
Lorraine Williams

Blueprints for

THE PARAGRAPH

Blueprints for the Paragraph

Objectives	In Part A, you will:
Analysis:	identify and analyze the three basic parts of a paragraph
Transitions:	learn to use *in addition (to), though* and *although,* and *later*
Practice:	paraphrase, summarize, and synthesize information

What Is a Paragraph?

A **paragraph** is a group of sentences that discusses one idea. Some paragraphs consist of two or three long sentences, but it is more common to have paragraphs of four to ten sentences of varied lengths. It is easy to recognize a paragraph because the first line is usually indented, or moved in, about five spaces or half an inch. Look at the first line of this paragraph, and you will see that it is indented. The space is called an **indentation**. If you count the number of indentations on a page, you will know the number of paragraphs on that page.

The Three Main Parts of a Paragraph

The basic organization of a paragraph is very simple. It has three main parts: the **topic sentence,** the **body** (which consists of supporting sentences), and the **concluding sentence.**

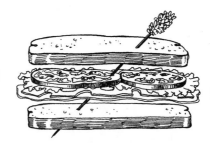

PARAGRAPH

Topic sentence

Body
(supporting sentences)

Concluding sentence

Topic Sentence

The topic sentence is a plan or guide for the reader. It tells the **topic** of your paragraph. Here is an example of a topic sentence:

Computer knowledge has improved the lives of many students.

The general topic of the paragraph is *computer knowledge.* A good topic sentence lets the reader know what your paragraph is about and sometimes how it is organized as well. Most of the time—but not always—the topic sentence is the first sentence of the paragraph.

In addition to a main topic, a topic sentence has a **controlling idea.** You use the controlling idea to develop the main topic in a particular direction. To find the controlling idea for the topic sentence above, ask a question about the topic: *What is important about computer knowledge?* The answer is that *it improves the lives of students,* and this is the controlling idea for the paragraph.

Consider these topic sentences, topics, and controlling ideas. Notice that the topic is the same in each topic sentence, but the controlling idea is different.

Topic sentence	Topic	Controlling idea
1. The quality of Hollywood movies has decreased in the last fifty years.	Hollywood movies	decreased quality
2. Hollywood movies are getting more expensive to produce for a number of reasons.	Hollywood movies	reasons for higher production costs
3. Hollywood movies are generally classified as comedies, action films, and romances.	Hollywood movies	three types: comedies, action films, and romances

Body

The main part of the paragraph is called the **body.** The sentences in the body *support* and add to the information in your topic sentence. Typically, there are four to eight supporting sentences in the body. All of these sentences must be about the same topic.

Here are two supporting sentences for the topic sentence about computers:

One way in which they make students' lives easier is by use of the Internet. Students can now find all sorts of information to aid in their research without leaving their homes.

Concluding Sentence

In the last sentence of your paragraph, you can sum up the contents and express your feelings. This sentence is called the **concluding sentence.** When you write only one paragraph about a topic, for example, you should always end with a concluding sentence.

Here is the concluding sentence for the paragraph about computers:

> *Students should be grateful that this new technology has made their studies so much easier.*

The writer includes the main topic and gives an opinion about this new technology.

If you are writing a few or several paragraphs about one topic, the purpose of the concluding sentence in each paragraph can be a little different. Sometimes the concluding sentence introduces the idea of the next paragraph. In other words, it acts as a transition sentence between ideas.

EXERCISE

1

IDENTIFYING THE THREE PARTS OF A PARAGRAPH (A)

Read the paragraph and answer the questions.

Selling a product successfully in another country often requires changes in the original product. Domino's Pizza offers mayonnaise and potato pizza in Tokyo and pickled ginger pizza in India. Heinz varies its ketchup recipe to satisfy the needs of specific markets. In Belgium and Holland, for example, the ketchup is not as sweet as it is in the United States. When Haagen-Dazs served up one of its most popular American flavors, Chocolate **Chip** Cookie **Dough,** to British customers, they left it sitting in supermarket freezers. What the **premium** ice cream maker learned is that chocolate chip cookies are not popular in Great Britain and

chip: a small piece

dough: a mixture of flour and liquids, butter, or oil

premium: top quality

(continued)

(continued)

snatch: take, grab

raw: uncooked

come up with: find, produce

dairy: milk products

wise: intelligent

fundamental: basic

that children do not have a history of **snatching raw** dough from the bowl, so the company had to develop flavors that would sell in Great Britain. After holding a contest to **come up with** a flavor the British would like, the company launched "Cool Britannia," vanilla ice cream with strawberries and chocolate-covered Scottish shortbread. Because **dairy** products are not part of Chinese diets, Frito-Lay took the cheese out of Chee-tos in China. Instead, the company sells Seafood Chee-tos. Without a doubt, these products were so successful in these foreign lands only because the company realized that it was **wise** to do market research and make **fundamental** changes in the products.

From *Business,* Sixth Edition, by Pride, Hughes, & Kapoor. Copyright © 1999
Houghton Mifflin Company. Reprinted with permission.

1. Write the topic sentence here. Circle the topic, and underline the controlling idea.

   _____

   _____

2. The body of this paragraph consists of many examples of how companies have modified their products in foreign markets. Underline the example that was the most unusual or surprising to you and explain why here.

   _____

   _____

3. Circle the concluding sentence. Which important ideas and terms are the same in both the topic sentence and the concluding sentence? Write some of them here.

   _____

   _____

EXERCISE

2

IDENTIFYING THE THREE PARTS OF A PARAGRAPH (B)

Read the paragraph and answer the questions.

I believe that capital punishment is wrong. First of all, there is the question of proving someone's guilt or innocence with 100 percent accuracy. What if a person who is judged as guilty is really innocent? We now know of many cases in the United States in which an innocent

(continued)

(continued)

permanent: forever

person was put to death. Because the result of capital punishment is **permanent,** it is important to be absolutely certain of a person's guilt. However, in some cases, this is simply not possible, so from time to time capital punishment will result in killing an innocent person. Second, capital punishment is killing. I do not believe in killing for any reason. Killing someone who may have killed someone else is not a solution. Finally, one reason given for capital punishment is that it is a deterrent. That is, some people believe that the fear of capital punishment will stop others from committing a murder. However, this is simply not true. If it were true, then we would have very few cases of capital punishment. History shows us that this has not been the case and that capital punishment has not been a **deterrent** to murder. For these and many other reasons, I cannot support capital punishment in any form.

deter: prevent, avoid

1. Write the topic sentence here. Circle the topic and underline the controlling idea.

   _____

   _____

2. The body of this paragraph consists of many reasons that capital punishment is wrong. Underline the example that was the most convincing to you. Then explain why here.

   _____

   _____

3. Circle the concluding sentence. Which important ideas and terms are the same in both the topic sentence and the concluding sentence? Write some of them here.

   _____

   _____

EXERCISE

3

IDENTIFYING THE THREE PARTS OF A PARAGRAPH (C)

Read the paragraph and answer the questions.

The most fundamental classification of the chemical elements is into two groups: metals and nonmetals. Metals typically have certain physical properties. For example, they have a shiny appearance. In addition, they have the ability to change shape without breaking, and they are excellent

(continued)

(continued)

conductor: carrier

yield: produce, result in

conductors of heat and electricity. Nonmetals, on the other hand, do not usually have these same physical properties. These three differences are important ones, but there are chemical differences between metals and nonmetals as well. When there is any doubt whether a chemical element is a metal or a nonmetal, a chemical analysis will **yield** the final answer. In sum, a careful consideration of the three physical properties and a chemical analysis are necessary to separate chemical elements into metals and nonmetals.

From *Introductory Chemistry* by Steven Zumdhal.
Copyright © 2000 Houghton Mifflin Company. Reprinted with permission.

1. Write the topic sentence here. Circle the topic, and underline the controlling idea.

   _____

   _____

2. The body of this paragraph consists of four ways in which metals and nonmetals differ. List these four differences here.

   _____

   _____

   _____

   _____

3. Circle the concluding sentence. Which important ideas and terms are the same in both the topic sentence and the concluding sentence? Write some of them here.

   _____

   _____

Sources: Reading and Analyzing Sample Paragraphs

In this section, you will read two paragraphs that are related in some way. You will study the structure of these paragraphs, understand their meanings, and eventually combine the two ideas to form your own paragraph.

SOURCE 1

Orlando: From Tiny Town to Major Metropolitan Area

PREREADING DISCUSSION QUESTIONS

1. *Make a list of the five most popular tourist places in the world. Why do people visit these places?*

2. *How big is your city? Imagine that twenty-five million tourists will visit your city every year starting next year. What benefits will this bring to your area? What problems will it create?*

EXERCISE

4

READING AND ANSWERING QUESTIONS

Read the paragraph about Orlando, Florida. Then answer the questions.

SOURCE 1

enormous: huge, tremendous

intensify: increase, grow

undergo: experience

given: considering

ORLANDO: FROM TINY TOWN TO MAJOR METROPOLITAN AREA

The city of Orlando, located in sunny central Florida, has experienced **enormous** growth and is now internationally known as a popular tourist destination. Founded in 1844, Orlando was a small town for more than a century. With the arrival of the South Florida Railroad in 1880, Orlando was on its way to rapid growth. However, no one could have predicted the extent of what was to come. This growth was **intensified** with the development of the Cape Canaveral space complex in 1950. Two decades later, Orlando experienced rapid growth again on an incredible scale when Walt Disney World opened its gates to tourists in 1971. Located twenty-two miles southwest of Orlando, the Disney complex alone covers some 28,000 acres. In addition to having Florida's largest hotel (with 1,509 rooms), Walt Disney World has a variety of thrilling attractions, including the Magic Kingdom, Epcot Center, Disney-MGM Studios, and Pleasure Island (an evening entertainment center). Though Orlando has other industries, the tourist industry is by far the leading source of employment for the region. Because of this increase in tourism, Orlando has **undergone** an amazing amount of growth, which will likely continue, **given** the popularity of this city as a world tourist destination.

Adapted from the Encylopedia Britannica © 2001 Britannica.com Inc.

1. What is the topic sentence of this paragraph? Write it here. Circle the topic, and underline the controlling idea.

   _____

   _____

   _____

2. Reread the body of the paragraph. Find examples of why tourists want to visit Orlando. These examples are the supporting facts for the topic sentence. Write them here.

   _____

   _____

   _____

   _____

3. Circle the concluding sentence. What ideas and terms do the topic sentence and the concluding sentence have in common? Write them here.

   _____

   _____

   _____

4. What ideas are different in the topic sentence and the concluding sentence? Write them here.

   _____

   _____

   _____

The Effects of Tourism on One Florida City

PREREADING DISCUSSION QUESTIONS

1. *Have you seen a town or city change dramatically because of development?*

2. *Have the changes been mostly positive or negative?*

3. *Do you prefer living in a city that is highly developed or in a more rural area? Why?*

READING AND ANSWERING QUESTIONS

Read the paragraph about Orlando, Florida. Then answer the questions.

THE EFFECTS OF TOURISM ON ONE FLORIDA CITY

Orlando, which was a quiet farming town a little more than thirty years ago, has more people passing through it today than any other place in the state of Florida. The reason, of course, is Walt Disney World, Universal Studios, Sea World, and **a host of** other theme attractions. These theme parks pull more than twenty-five million people a year to what was until **fairly** recently an empty area of land. Few of these people visit the actual city of Orlando. Instead, they prefer to stay in one of the countless motels and hotels fifteen miles to the south along Highway 19 or five miles southwest on International Drive. Despite enormous expansion over the last decade, the city itself remains free of the commercialism that surrounds it. However, the city has not been able to escape the traffic congestion and other problems associated with the visit of so many millions of tourists **as well as** the thousands of people who work in the tourist industry. Without a doubt, tourism has certainly changed life for the residents of Orlando and the surrounding area.

a host of: a number of

fairly: rather, more or less

as well as: and, in addition to

POSTREADING DISCUSSION QUESTIONS

1. *Are Source 1 and Source 2 about the same topic? If so, what is the topic?*

2. *Subtopics are the smaller topics in a paragraph that add information related to the main topic. For example, in Source 1, one subtopic is the history of Orlando's growth. Do the two sources include the same subtopics? What are the subtopics in Source 1? In Source 2?*

3. *In your opinion, which one of the sources is better organized? Explain your opinion.*

EXERCISE

THE THREE PARTS OF A PARAGRAPH

1. What is the topic sentence? Write it here. Circle the topic, and underline the controlling idea.

    _____

    _____

2. Reread the body of the paragraph. What two things does the writer say about the city (as compared to the tourist areas)?

    _____

    _____

    _____

3. Circle the concluding sentence. What ideas and terms do the topic sentence and the concluding sentence have in common? Write them here.

    _____

    _____

    _____

4. Find any important differences in the content of the topic sentence and the content of the concluding sentence. Write them here.

    _____

    _____

    _____

Transition Expressions

Writers use transition expressions to connect sentences and ideas. Transition expressions are words and phrases that help your ideas flow and make them sound logical to readers.

There are many transition expressions in English, such as *but, in addition, for these reasons,* and *on the other hand.* You will study a few transition expressions in each unit of this book.

Unit 1 Transition Expressions: *in addition (to), though* and *although, later*

(continued)

(continued)

in addition (to)

Function: Adds information.

Uses: *In addition to* is a preposition, and what follows it must be a noun or pronoun.

Example: In addition to *chocolate pie,* we love chocolate ice cream.

Practice: Find a sentence in Source 1 (page 8) that contains *in addition to*. Write it here.

_____

though and although

Function: Shows contrast or shows that a fact is not important; *though* and *although* have a similar meaning and use.

Use: Both *though* and *although* introduce a dependent clause, so a subject and a verb must follow.

Examples: Though (OR Although) Victor dislikes the taste of coffee, he likes the smell.

Though (OR Although) May is usually cool, this May has been warm.

Practice: Find a sentence in Source 1 (page 8) that contains *though* or *although*. Write it here.

_____

later

Function: To help show events in a sequence, to introduce something that happens after something else.

Use: *Later* is often preceded by or followed by time expressions that make it more specific. Some examples are *a few weeks later, several days later,* and *later that day.*

Examples: He ate breakfast with his cousin. Later that day, he met with me.

She went on vacation to Hawaii. A few weeks later, she returned.

Practice: Find a sentence in Source 1 (page 8) that contains *later*. Write it here.

_____

(continued)

WORKING WITH TRANSITION EXPRESSIONS

Fill in the blanks with later, in addition (to), or though or although.

1. In 2000, Julia Roberts won an Oscar for Best Actress in the popular movie *Erin Brockovich*. _____ she had received nominations, including Best Supporting Actress for *Steel Magnolias* in 1989 and *Pretty Woman* in 1990, she had not won an Oscar. In fact, it was not until ten years later that Julia won her first Oscar for her amazing portrayal of a young, twice-divorced mother of two who was trying to make a living in the world.

2. _____ these three movies, audiences around the world know Julia for her roles in *My Best Friend's Wedding*, *Sleeping with the Enemy*, and *The Pelican Brief*.

3. Julia Roberts was born in Georgia in 1967. At the age of seventeen, she left her home state and headed to New York, where her sister was working as an actress. Julia started out as a model. _____, she took some acting classes. Her big break occurred when her brother, actor Eric Roberts, persuaded a director to let Julia work in the movie *Blood Red*.

4. While many fans know Julia's movies, few of them know that her real name was Julie. She used this name in her early movies. _____, she changed her name from Julie to Julia because there was already an actress named Julie Roberts.

5. _____ she has starred in numerous films that have done well at the box office, the role that convinced many people to pay attention to this actress was her portrayal of a prostitute in *Pretty Woman*. Costarring with Richard Gere, Julia captured the hearts of millions of moviegoers.

Paraphrasing, Summarizing, and Synthesizing

In academic writing, you will often have to write information based on something you have read. Therefore, it is important to learn how to **paraphrase** (use different language to say the same thing), **summarize** (express the same idea in fewer words), and **synthesize** (combine information from two or more sources) to answer a specific question of interest.

Study the diagram below. It shows how you may paraphrase a source, summarize a source, and then use these skills to synthesize information from two or more sources into your original writing.

PARAPHRASING:

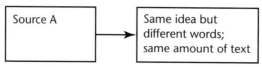

SUMMARIZING:

SYNTHESIZING:

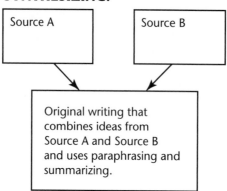

Paraphrasing: An Important Composition Skill

When you write a paragraph, you use your original ideas and information that you have learned through experience. In addition, you often use information from print and electronic sources such as books, web sites, magazines, and newspapers.

You can use such source information in two ways. Both ways show that you borrowed this information.

1. Put quotation marks around the exact words.

Example:

According to a report in the *New England Journal of Medicine,* "Senior citizens who have experienced acute chest pains at least twice in the past six months often find themselves back in the hospital within a month if they have not sought professional treatment."

2. **Paraphrase,** or restate, another writer's words and ideas in your own words.

Example:

The *New England Journal of Medicine* reported that elderly patients who have suffered chest pains two times in six months must get medical treatment or they may end up in the hospital within thirty days.

CAREFUL! In both of these examples, you need to avoid plagiarism and use parenthetical documentation to tell where you found the original material. (See Appendix 1 for information about documenting sources.)

A good paraphrase gives the same ideas and information as the original sentence but in different words. As the example above shows, the length of the paraphrase may be similar to the original, but the grammar is usually not the same. Key vocabulary, which may be technical, is often the same because there might not be another way to state it.

IMPORTANT NOTE:

How do you introduce information from an outside source? One way is to use the phrase *according to* followed by the author's name or the name of the book.

Example: <u>According to</u> a report in the *New England Journal of Medicine,* . . . (your paraphrase)

Another way is to use the name of the source with a verb that indicates a sharing of information such as *state, say, argue, believe, reveal, conclude, report,* or *suggest.*

Example: The *New England Journal of Medicine* <u>reported</u> that . . . (your paraphrase)

A Few Facts About Plagiarism

Plagiarism is passing off someone else's writing and ideas as your own. It is a serious issue in academic circles. If you turn in an assignment that you did not write, you can suffer terrible consequences such as academic probation or even expulsion from a college or university.

Plagiarism is not always intentional. Sometimes you find information from a book, an article, or a web site that you believe is excellent support for your paragraph. However, if you do not put quotation marks around the exact words or paraphrase the information, you are in effect stealing the intellectual property of the original writer. To use source materials correctly and avoid plagiarism, learn the skills of paraphrasing, summarizing, and synthesizing and then apply correct documentation format. (See Appendix 1 for information about documenting sources.)

Note to Advanced Students

In English, the verbs that are used to name a source (*state, say, argue, believe, reveal, conclude, report, suggest*) are sometimes used in the present tense rather than the past tense. However, the meaning does not change at all.

Examples: The *New York Times* <u>states</u> that Mayor Giuliani wants to serve an unprecedented third term.

The investigator <u>believes</u> that the ship's captain is responsible for the accident.

Examples of Paraphrasing

Paraphrasing is an extremely important skill for all academic writers. Study these examples of good and bad paraphrasing.

Original (13 words)

Selling a product successfully in another country often requires changes in the original product.

Main idea to keep:

Companies must change their products to succeed in another country

---

Good paraphrase (15 words)

The most successful exporting companies have succeeded because they made important changes in their products.

1. *It keeps the idea that change is necessary.*
2. *Grammar is different (subject:* exporting companies; *verb:* have succeeded; *dependent clause:* because they made important changes in their products*).*
3. *Vocabulary is different (*successful exporting companies, have succeeded because, important*).*
4. *Length is similar to original.*

Poor paraphrase (14 words)

To sell a product successfully in another country, you need to change the product.

1. *The ideas are the same, but the wording is too similar (*successfully, in another country*). In fact, it is almost exactly the same. (Reread the original above.) *This is plagiarism!*
2. *Though the length is similar to the original, only minor changes were made (*Selling = To sell; often requires = you need to*)*

EXERCISE

7

PARAPHRASING: MULTIPLE CHOICE

*Read the original sentence. Then read the three possible paraphrases. Mark one **B** (BEST), one **TS** (TOO SIMILAR), and one **D** (DIFFERENT—or wrong—information).*

SOURCE
1
Page 8

1. *With the arrival of the South Florida Railroad in 1880, Orlando was on its way to rapid growth.*

_____ A. The city of Orlando began to grow tremendously when the South Florida Railroad reached the city in 1880.

_____ B. With the arrival of the South Florida Railroad in 1880, the city of Orlando was on its way to fast growth.

_____ C. Most people were genuinely shocked at how quickly Orlando grew after the South Florida Railroad arrived in 1880.

SOURCE
2
Page 10

2. *These theme parks pull more than twenty-five million people a year to what was until recently an empty area of land.*

_____ A. The theme parks in Orlando attract over twenty-five million people every year, and this area was empty until recently.

_____ B. Because the theme parks in the Orlando area are so popular, there is no more space for additional parks.

_____ C. Over twenty-five million tourists visit this recently developed Florida city because of its numerous theme parks.

EXERCISE

8

PARAPHRASING PRACTICE

Read these original sentences from Source 1 and Source 2. Circle what you consider to be the most important ideas. Then in number 1, choose the best paraphrase for the original sentence(s). In number 2, write your own paraphrase of the sentence(s).

SOURCE
1
Page 8

1. *Two decades later, Orlando experienced rapid growth again on an incredible scale when Walt Disney World opened its gates to tourists in 1971.*

_____ A. Twenty years later, rapid growth on an incredible scale was seen in Orlando when Walt Disney World opened its gates to tourists.

_____ B. In 1971, Walt Disney World opened for business in Orlando.

_____ C. The opening of Walt Disney World in 1971 caused a massive increase in the number of tourists to Orlando.

SOURCE
2
Page 10

2. *Orlando, which was a quiet farming town a little more than thirty years ago, has more people passing through it than any other place in the state of Florida.*

Your paraphrase:

_____

_____

_____

Summarizing

Remember that quoting and paraphrasing are techniques you can use to include information from another source in your writing. A third way to include information from another source is by **summarizing** it. A summary is a shortened version, in your own words, of someone else's ideas. These ideas may come from an article, a book, or a lecture. In college courses, knowing how to write summaries can be useful. For example, you may be asked to answer a test question with a short paragraph that summarizes the key points in your lecture notes. Before you can write a research paper, you will need to summarize the main ideas in your sources of information. When you summarize, you do not include all of the information from the source. Instead, you use only the parts you think are the most important and paraphrase them, or put them in your own words.

Summarizing involves not only writing, but also reading and critical thinking. To summarize, you should do the following.

GUIDELINES FOR SUMMARIZING

1. Read the source material and understand it well.

2. Decide which parts of the source material are the most important.

3. Put the important parts in the same order they appear in the original.

4. Paraphrase (see p. 14)—use different grammar and vocabulary. You must write information in your own words.

5. If the original states a point and then gives multiple examples, include a general statement with one example instead of all the examples.

6. Use verbs that indicate that you are summarizing information from a source (and not from your own head) such as *suggest, report, argue, tell, say, ask, question,* or *conclude.*

A summary is always shorter than the original writing. A ten-page article might become a few paragraphs in a summary. A 200-page book might become an essay.

Summarizing is a very important skill for a good writer. It is especially important when you are taking information from long sources. Study these examples of good and poor summarizing.

Original (190 words)

Selling a product successfully in another country often requires changes in the original product. Domino's Pizza offers mayonnaise and potato pizza in Tokyo and pickled ginger pizza in India. Heinz varies its ketchup recipe to satisfy the needs of specific markets. In Belgium and Holland, for example, the ketchup is not as sweet as it is in the United States. When Haagen-Dazs served up one of its most popular American flavors, Chocolate Chip Cookie Dough, to British customers, they left it sitting in supermarket freezers. What the premium ice-cream maker learned is that chocolate chip cookies are not popular in Great Britain and that children do not have a history of snatching raw dough from the bowl, so the company had to develop flavors that would sell in Great Britain. After holding a contest to come up with a flavor the British would like, the company launched "Cool Britannia," vanilla ice cream with strawberries and chocolate-covered Scottish shortbread. Because dairy products are not part of Chinese diets, Frito-Lay took the cheese out of Chee-tos in China. Instead, the company sells Seafood Chee-tos. Without a doubt, these products were so successful in these foreign lands only because the company realized that it was wise to do market research and make fundamental changes in the products.

Main ideas:

1. Companies must change their products to succeed.
2. Examples of companies that did this: Domino's, Heinz, Haagen-Dazs, Frito-Lay.

Good Summary (36 words):

Companies must adapt their products if they want to do well in foreign markets. Many well-known companies, including Domino's, Heinz, Haagen-Dazs, and Frito-Lay, have altered their products and proved this point.

1. It covers the main ideas.
2. It is a true summary, not an exact repeat of the specific examples.
3. It includes some new grammar, for example: Original text: often requires changes

Summary: Modal is used: *"companies **must** choose"*

4. It includes some new vocabulary, for example:
Original text: *Specific company names*
Summary: *"many well-known companies"*

Poor Summary (187 words)

Changes in a product are important if a company wants to sell it successfully in another country. For example, Domino's Pizza offers mayonnaise and potato pizza in Tokyo and pickled ginger pizza in India. In addition, Heinz has changed its ketchup recipe to satisfy the needs of specific markets. In Belgium and Holland the ketchup is less sweet. When Haagen-Dazs served up one of its most popular American flavors, Chocolate Chip Cookie Dough, to British customers, the British customers left it sitting in supermarket freezers. The luxury ice-cream maker learned that chocolate chip cookies are not popular in Great Britain, and children do not take uncooked dough from the bowl. For this reason, the company flavors to sell in Great Britain. Since dairy products are not usually eaten in China, Frito-Lay removed the cheese from Chee-tos in China. In its place, the company has Seafood Chee-tos. Certainly, these items were so successful in these countries only because the company was smart enough to do market research and implement fundamental changes in the products.

1. It is almost as long as the original and, therefore, not really a summary.
2. It includes almost the same vocabulary, for example:
Original text: *the premium ice-cream maker*
Summary: *the luxury ice-cream maker* <u>This is plagiarism!</u>
3. It includes almost the same grammar, for example:
Original text: *For this reason, the company had to develop flavors that would sell in Great Britain.*
Summary: *For this reason, the company developed flavors to sell in Great Britain.* <u>This is plagiarism!</u>

EXERCISE

9

SUMMARIZING: IDENTIFYING THE MOST IMPORTANT IDEAS

Reread Source 2 (page 10). Then do the following:

1. *Make a list of at least four important facts and ideas.*

2. *Paraphrase these facts and ideas.*

3. *Use phrases, not complete sentences.*

1. _____

_____

2. _____

_____

3. _____

_____

4. _____

_____

EXERCISE

10

SUMMARIZING: PUTTING IT IN YOUR OWN WORDS

Using your ideas from Exercise 9, write two to five sentences that summarize the original message of Source 2 (page 10).

_____

_____

_____

_____

_____

_____

_____

_____

_____

_____

_____

Synthesizing

A synthesis is a combination of information from two or more sources. When you synthesize, you take information from different sources and blend them smoothly into your paragraph.

BASIC STEPS FOR SYNTHESIZING

1. Read the material from all of the sources.

2. Choose the important ideas from each source. To do this, you must analyze the information. Ask yourself, "What is the author's purpose for writing this information?" Then decide which pieces of information are most important in accomplishing what the author intends. It is always important in synthesizing to use only the important, relevant information.

3. Group together the ideas that are connected and that support each other.

4. Combine the ideas in each group into sentences, using your paraphrasing skills. You must write information in your own words.

5. Organize the sentences logically, and combine them into one continuous piece of writing. Do not forget to include your original ideas, too.

6. Check your work for accuracy and smoothness. Add transition words where they are needed.

Synthesis is an important skill for academic writers, who often use more than one source when writing papers. Study these examples of good and poor synthesizing.

Source A (81 words)

Switzerland has a great example of linguistic diversity because there are three different national languages. People in the central and northern areas speak German. People in the western area speak French. People in the southeastern area of the country speak Italian. Most Swiss can speak more than one language. One interesting fact is that the name of the country on its coins and stamps is not in any of these languages. Instead, "Helvetia," the Latin name for this country, is used.
Claudio Acevedo, Argentina

Main ideas to keep:
1. Geographical areas of Switzerland speak different languages.
2. Central and northern regions = German
3. Western part = French, southeastern region = Italian
4. The Latin name for Switzerland is used as well.

Source B (54 words)

You might think that most of the people in Switzerland speak the same language because it is a rather small country. However, you would be wrong. Yes, the country is tiny, but there are four national languages. German is spoken by more people than any other language. The second most commonly spoken language is French, and Italian is third. A very small percentage of the people speak Romansch.
Najmuddin bin Faisal, Malaysia

Main ideas to keep:
Most Swiss speak German, then French, then Italian, and finally a few people in Switzerland speak Romansch.

Good synthesis (116 words)

Although Switzerland is a small country, several languages are spoken there. In fact, this tiny country has four national languages. The most commonly spoken language is German, which is used in the central and northern regions. The second most widely spoken language is French, which is used in the western area of the country. The third most commonly used language is Italian, which is spoken in the southeastern area of Switzerland. A fourth language, Romansch, is spoken by only a very small percentage of the population.

1. It has ideas from both sources (for example, *Source A:* German is spoken in the central and northern regions; *Source B:* the most common language is German)
2. The ideas are woven together. (The most commonly spoken language is German, which is used in the central and northern regions.)
3. The sequence of the material is logical. (first, second, third, fourth most common languages)

Interestingly, the name for Switzerland on Swiss currency is not in any of these languages. Instead, Helvetia, the Latin term for this country, is used.

Poor synthesis (88 words)

Switzerland is tiny, but there are four national languages. The languages in order of usage are German, French, Italian, and Romansch. Portuguese and Greek are not spoken in this country. People in the western area speak French. People in the southeastern area of the country speak Italian. People in the central and northern areas speak German. One interesting fact is that the name of the country on its coins and stamps is not in any of these languages. Instead, "Helvetia," the Latin name for this country, is used.

1. The ideas are not woven together very well. It is easy to see where one source ends and another begins. Source 2 information ends after The languages in order of usage are: German, French, Italian, and Romansch. Source 1 information takes up the rest of the paragraph.
2. The third sentence is an unrelated idea about Portuguese and Greek that is not from either source.
3. The sequence of the languages by geographical areas is illogical because it does not match the list of languages given at the beginning of the paragraph.

EXERCISE

11

SYNTHESIZING: EXAM QUESTION PRACTICE

Imagine that you are a student in a sociology class. In a paragraph of four to eight sentences, write your answer to the exam question below. Synthesize the information from Source 1 and Source 2 about Orlando, Florida. The following diagram will remind you of the synthesizing process.

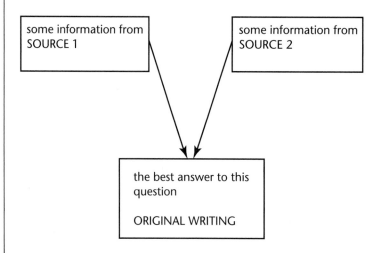

SOCIOLOGY EXAM QUESTION:

Discuss how the tourist industry has affected Orlando, Florida. Briefly describe the history of the city and tell what events influenced its growth. Explain how the tourist industry has affected the people of Orlando both positively and negatively.

_____

_____

_____

_____

_____

_____

_____

_____

_____

_____

_____

_____

_____

_____

_____

_____

_____

_____

_____

_____

The Writing Process: Practice Writing Paragraphs

Objectives	In Part B, you will:
Prewriting:	brainstorm ideas about a topic
Planning:	(1) ask questions as a way to organize ideas; (2) use an outline
First draft:	learn the correct formatting for a paragraph
Partner feedback:	review classmates' paragraphs and analyze feedback
Second draft:	use partner feedback to write a second draft
Editing:	
Grammar Focus:	write both singular and plural forms of count nouns
Sentence Check:	practice writing complete sentences that always include a verb
Mechanics:	use commas with certain transition words
Final draft:	complete the final draft of a paragraph

The Writing Process: Writing Assignment

Your assignment is to write an original paragraph of five to ten sentences describing your favorite vacation. The vacation can be real or imaginary. Follow the steps in the writing process in this section.

Prewriting: Brainstorming

Brainstorming can help writers get ideas before they write. You can brainstorm with a group or a partner, or you can brainstorm by yourself. To brainstorm, think of as many ideas as possible about a topic. Write the ideas as they come to you without evaluating, connecting, or editing them.

Write Ideas Quickly

For this assignment, brainstorm about three or four of your favorite vacations or about vacations in general. Write quickly whatever comes to mind: where you went, when you went, what you did, how you felt, and so on. Do not worry about the importance or sequence of your ideas for now. Just try to think of as many ideas as you can. Remember that you can include imaginary vacations, too. Here is a sample brainstorming.

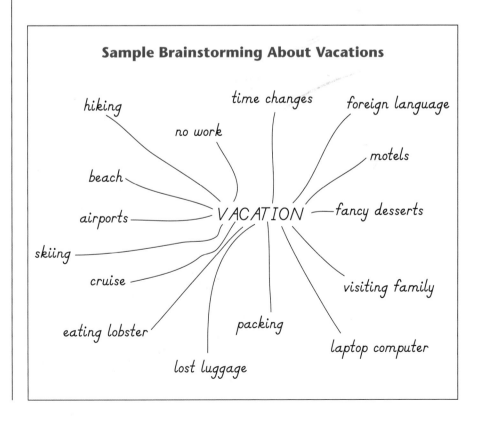

Now try brainstorming about a vacation in the box below. Do not worry about using complete sentences or correct grammar. This exercise should help you get ideas for your paragraph.

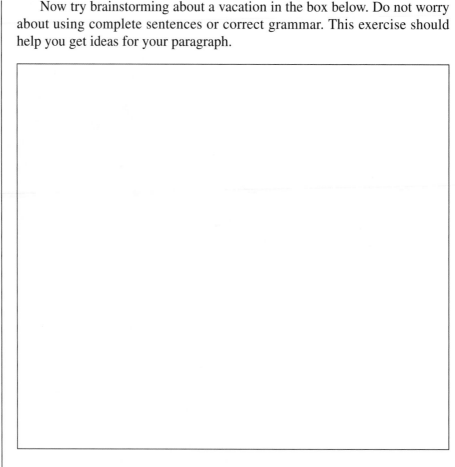

Write More About a Specific Vacation

Next, look at the ideas you wrote. Use them to decide which vacation you will write a paragraph about. To do this, ask yourself some questions:

1. Which vacation was the most memorable?

2. Which vacation can you write the most about? Remember you will be writing five to ten sentences.

3. Which vacation was so good that you would like to experience it again?

Once you choose a specific vacation, you can answer more questions about it and continue brainstorming.

▶ Where did you go?

▶ When did you go?

▶ Whom did you go with?

▶ What transportation did you use?

▶ Was it your first time there?

▶ How long were you there?

▶ Did you have a good time?

▶ What are some things that you did there?

▶ Is there anything now that reminds you of that place when you see it, hear it, or smell it?

▶ If you had a chance, would you go back?

Planning: Lists and Outlining

Make a List

The next step is to plan and organize your ideas. You will also generate more ideas in this step. An easy way to organize is to first make a simple list of the most important information from your brainstorming. Feel free to add new information as necessary. Fill in the blanks below about your vacation.

Time: _____

Travel companions: _____

Mode of travel: _____

First time there? _____

Who decided on the trip? _____

Length of stay: _____

Have a good time? _____

Activities: _____

What was your favorite? _____

Is there anything that reminds you of that place now when you see it, hear it, or smell it?

_____

_____

How would you rate your desire to return and why?

_____

_____

Make an Outline

Now reread the information you filled out in the list above. Choose the information that you want to include in your vacation paragraph. Remember that you do not have to use all the information. Study the outline below as an example.

TOPIC SENTENCE: _____

A. Where/when/with whom
   1. Orlando
   2. 1999
   3. With family

B. Describe the trip
   1. Planning
      a. Rental car
      b. Hotel
      c. Itinerary

   2. Activities
      a. Weather
      b Different parks

   3. How do I feel about it now?
      a. It was the best trip!
      b. I would like to go again.

Now write an outline of your vacation paragraph.

_____

_____

_____

_____

_____

_____

_____

_____

_____

_____

_____

_____

_____

_____

First Draft

You are now ready to write the first draft of your paragraph. Many writers begin with the topic sentence. Review your list and outline in the previous section, then write your topic sentence here:

_____

_____

_____

If you cannot think of a topic sentence right now, write a few sentences about the details of your vacation. As you write these details, you may think of a more general sentence to use as a topic sentence, for example, *My trip to Brice Canyon in Utah was the most adventurous vacation I have ever taken.* With a topic sentence like this, all your supporting sentences would show how the trip was an adventure.

Paragraph Format

Now is a good time to learn the format of a paragraph. You can then refer to this section when you write other paragraphs in this book.

When you write your paragraph, follow these paragraph-formatting rules.

The Format of a Paragraph

1. Give your paragraph a title, and write it in the center of the top line.

2. Double-space your paragraph to make it easier to read.

3. Indent the first line.

4. Leave a one-inch margin on all sides.

5. Write continuously and do not start each sentence on a new line. (In word processing, do not use a hard return at the end of a sentence.)

6. Begin each sentence with a capital letter.

7. End each sentence with correct punctuation.

8. Be sure to have a topic sentence.

9. Write three to eight supporting sentences.

10. End with a concluding sentence.

PARAGRAPH FORMAT

Read the paragraph. Write the format rule labels on the lines.

1. _____

2. _____

3. _____

4. _____

5. _____

6. _____

7. _____

My Best Vacation

<u>I will never forget the excellent trip I took to Orlando, Florida.</u> My parents, my brother, and I decided to go there in the summer of 1999. The four of us flew from our hometown of Denver to Orlando. When we arrived in Orlando, we got a rental car and drove to our hotel. After dinner, we planned our itinerary for the next three days. The weather was great the whole week, and I had the time of my life! We visited the Magic Kingdom, Epcot Center, Universal, and Animal Kingdom. Each park was different from the others, and we had an incredible time at each one. <u>I have taken several trips since that summer of 1999, but the best trip in my life was my trip to Orlando!</u>

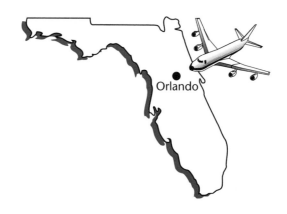

Orlando

First Draft

Now write the first draft of your paragraph on separate paper. When you finish, use this checklist to review your writing.

First Draft Checklist

1. Do I have a topic sentence that contains a clear topic and controlling idea?

2. Are all the sentences about the topic?

3. Are the sentences in a logical order?

4. Did I include transition words to help the reader?

5. Does my concluding sentence summarize the paragraph or express feelings?

6. Did I format my paragraph correctly?

Guidelines for Partner Feedback

Here are some guidelines about how to listen and talk to your partner about his or her work:

▶ Begin by saying something positive about the paragraph.

▶ Be specific about what works well and about what needs work.

▶ Find a straightforward but polite way to suggest improvements to the writing.

▶ When it is your turn to listen, take notes about how to revise your paragraph on the basis of your partner's feedback.

▶ Do not interrupt when your partner is talking. Try to save your response until he or she is finished speaking.

Peer Review

Exchange papers with another student. Read your partner's paper, and answer the questions on Partner Feedback Form: Unit 1, pp. 193–194. Discuss your partner's reactions to your paragraph. Make notes about any parts you need to change in your second draft.

Second Draft

Second draft revising should include more than grammar, punctuation, and spelling corrections. You should also be checking the topic sentence, the supporting details, the concluding sentence, and the overall completeness and clarity of your paragraph. Now carefully revise your paragraph using feedback from your partner and your own ideas for revising.

Second Draft Checklist

1. Is my topic sentence easy for the reader to understand?

2. Does the topic sentence give an idea of what the paragraph is about?

3. Are all the sentences about this topic? Is there any sentence that does not belong here?

4. Is there any sentence that seems out of order?

5. How many transition expressions are there? (Underline them.)

6. Have I considered all my partner's comments and suggestions?

Editing: Grammar and Mechanics

Now that your paragraph has taken shape and the content is clear, it is time to edit for grammar and mechanics (punctuation). In this part of the unit, you will look at two kinds of grammar as well as mechanics. The first grammar instruction, Grammar Focus, highlights English grammar points that are common problems for English-as-a-second-language students. The second grammar instruction, Sentence Check, will help you write better sentences and, therefore, better paragraphs.

Grammar Focus: Singular and Plural Nouns

1 Remember that a count noun can be counted (*brick, bicycle, shoe*). When you write a singular count noun, make sure it has one of the following elements in front of it.

- ▶ An article—*a, an, the*
- ▶ A demonstrative form—*this, that*
- ▶ A possessive form—*John's, Pamela's, my, his, her*

Incorrect   Hillary Clinton became senator in 2001.

Correct: Hillary Clinton became **a** senator in 2001.

Incorrect: The mayor is angry because there is lack of funds for new roads in plan. To some, the reason for problem is obvious.

Correct: The mayor is angry because there is **a** lack of funds for new roads in **his** plan. To some, the reason for **this** problem is obvious.

2 Most plural count nouns end in *-s*. Some clues that indicate a plural noun is needed are *some, many, a few, these, those, numerous, a number of, all, most,* and *various*.

Incorrect: Those fund will pay for various project that the mayor wants to start.

Correct: Those **funds** will pay for various **projects** that the mayor wants to start.

Incorrect: At last week's meeting, many citizen voiced their opposition to those recent decision.

Correct: At last week's meeting, many **citizens** voiced their opposition to those recent **decisions.**

EXERCISE 13

GRAMMAR: EDITING FOR SINGULAR AND PLURAL COUNT NOUNS

Some of the underlined nouns in the sentences below are correct and some are incorrect. Correct the errors and be prepared to explain why you did or did not change the nouns.

1. According to the mayor's recently released <u>plan</u>, one part of the city will undergo a major <u>changes</u> in the next few <u>months</u>.

2. Though this <u>changes</u> is supposedly for the best overall, many <u>resident</u> are of course upset by the plan because they may be relocated to other <u>places</u>.

3. The <u>parts</u> of the city that the <u>mayor</u>'s plan affects directly is the <u>area</u> between the river on the west and Highway 50 on the east.

4. All of the <u>residences</u> located in this <u>areas</u> of the city will have to be demolished to make way for a new shopping <u>centers</u>.

5. Whether or not this <u>plans</u> is realistic remains to be seen, but the mayor certainly has a great deal of support from the business community because this new shopping <u>center</u> could bring in over two <u>millions</u> dollars every <u>months</u>.

EXERCISE 14

GRAMMAR: CHOOSE SINGULAR OR PLURAL NOUNS

Fill in each blank with the correct singular or plural form of the noun in parentheses. Look for language clues about singular and plural (see Grammar Focus, p. 34).

I believe that capital punishment is wrong. First of all, there is the question of guilt or innocence. What if the person is really innocent? We now know of many **1.** (case) _____ in the United States in which an innocent **2.** (person) _____ was put to death. Because the result of capital punishment is permanent, it is important to be 100 percent sure of a person's guilt. However, in some **3.** (case) _____, this is simply not possible, so capital punishment will result in killing innocent **4.** (human) _____ from time to time. Second, capital punishment is killing. I do not believe in killing for any reason. Killing someone who may have killed someone else is not a valid

5. (solution) _____. Finally, one of the **6.** (reason) _____ that many people cite for having capital punishment is that it is a **7.** (deterrent) _____. That is, the fear of capital punishment will stop people from committing a **8.** (murder) _____. However, this is simply not true. If it were true, then we would have very few **9.** (case) _____ of capital punishment. History shows us that this has not been the case and that capital punishment has not been a deterrent to murder. For these and many other **10.** (reason) _____, I cannot support capital punishment in any form.

Sentence Check: Include a Verb in Every Sentence

A sentence is a collection of words that expresses a complete thought. Each English sentence must have a **verb.** Examples of verbs are *go, is, took, wondered,* and *pretends.* Always check every sentence to make sure that it includes a verb.

Because verbs go with subjects, you should then check for the subject. Remember that the subject of an English sentence is the person or thing that does the action of the main verb. (Ask: *who or what does the action of the verb?* The answer is the subject of the sentence.)

Incorrect:	Calcutta, with more than fourteen million people, the largest city in India. (no verb)
Correct:	Calcutta, with more than fourteen million people, **is** the largest city in India.
Incorrect:	In 1911, at the young age of twenty-five, Niels Bohr his Ph.D. degree in physics. (no verb)
Correct:	In 1911, at the young age of twenty-five, Niels Bohr **received** his Ph.D. degree in physics.
Incorrect:	From 1861 to his death in 1865, everyone the name of Abraham Lincoln. (no verb)
Correct:	From 1861 to his death in 1865, everyone **knew** the name of Abraham Lincoln.

EXERCISE

15

GRAMMAR: MISSING VERBS

The following paragraph is missing some verbs. Insert the following verbs in the correct places.

has	is
come	add
produce	are
grows	needs

caladium

    The caladium is a popular garden plant because it ∧*grows* quickly, is easy to take care of, and comes in a variety of colors. To grow well, it water and a warm climate. The caladium is rather small. At its peak, it reaches only 18 inches in height, which is approximately 46 centimeters. Its heart-shaped leaves in a variety of colors, but a basic color found in each variety is green. In fact, the most common variety the one with dark green leaves. This particular variety a deep red center. Though the caladium with dark green leaves is the most common type, there many other varieties. These other varieties leaves that are white, pink, or speckled. A few caladiums can certainly a lot of color to any garden. For these important reasons, the caladium is popular with gardeners.

EXERCISE

16

GRAMMAR: LOOKING FOR THE VERB

Read this paragraph and look for sentences that are missing verbs. Add appropriate verbs.

    The most fundamental classification of the chemical elements is into two groups: metals and nonmetals. Metals typically certain physical properties. For example, they have a shiny appearance. In addition, they the ability to change shape without breaking, and they have excellent conductivity of heat and electricity. Nonmetals, on the other hand, do not usually have these same physical properties. These three differences important, but there are chemical differences between metals and nonmetals that interest us more. When there is any doubt whether a chemical element is a metal or a nonmetal, a chemical analysis will yield the final answer. In sum, a careful consideration of the three physical properties and a chemical analysis necessary to separate chemical elements into metals and nonmetals.

Mechanics: Commas with Transition Words

When transition expressions such as *in addition (to), (al)though,* and *later* appear at the beginning of a sentence, a comma is required after the phrase that the transition word begins.

Examples:	*in addition to*	<u>In addition to</u> the house, he bought the car.
	(al)though	<u>Although</u> she hit the brakes, she did not stop in time.
	later	<u>Later</u> that same morning, he met with me.

When the transition words occur in the middle of a sentence, generally no comma is required.

Examples:	*in addition to*	He bought the car <u>in addition to</u> the house.
	(al)though	She did not stop in time <u>though</u> she hit the brakes.
	later	He met with me <u>later</u> that same morning.

MECHANICS: COMMAS WITH TRANSITIONS

Add the correct punctuation. Sometimes more than one answer is possible, and sometimes no punctuation is needed. You should be able to explain your answers.

1. She was first known as a famous child actress. Later in her life Shirley Temple Black became U.S. Ambassador to Ghana.

2. Mrs. Wills can speak Greek and Italian in addition to Afrikaans.

3. Orlando is a well-known international tourist destination. Though millions of tourists visit the area each year relatively few of them stay in the city of Orlando.

4. Though no one has come forth as a witness police believe that someone might have seen the car on Friday, July 17th.

5. In the 2000 U.S. presidential election, the winner was not known immediately. An exact count of the votes was finally available several weeks later.

6. In addition to teaching French Dr. Lorraine can be found counseling students.

Return to Your Second Draft

Now look at your second draft again and check these items. Make corrections where necessary.

Second Draft Checklist II

1. Did you use singular and plural nouns correctly?

2. Does each sentence contain a verb?

3. Check carefully for run-on sentences, comma splices, and fragments. (See Appendix 2, Appendix 3, and Appendix 4 for more information on these three sentence problems.)

4. Have you used the transitions *in addition (to), although, though,* or *later*? If so, are they correctly punctuated?

Final Draft

Carefully revise your paragraph using all of the feedback you have received: partner feedback review, instructor comments, and self-evaluation. In addition, try reading your paragraph aloud. This can help you find awkward-sounding sentences and errors in punctuation. When you have finished, neatly type your final draft.

Additional Writing Assignments from the Academic Disciplines

Beginning with the prewriting activity on page 27, go through the writing process and write another paragraph. Choose a topic from the following list.

SUBJECT	WRITING TASK
Science	Write about a giraffe. Discuss its body (size, shape, markings, horns). What makes a giraffe unique?
Computers	Discuss this idea: In one generation, the Internet will change education more than any other innovation in the past century.
Business	Choose a company or business that you know. Why is this business so successful?
Architecture	Describe the White House in Washington, D.C., and discuss its history.

UNIT
2

Blueprints for

DESCRIPTIVE
PARAGRAPHS

PART A # Blueprints for Descriptive Paragraphs

Objectives	In Part A, you will:
Analysis:	identify the key features of descriptive writing
Transitions:	learn to use *when, while, as,* and *after*
Practice:	paraphrase, summarize, and synthesize information

What Is a Descriptive Paragraph?

When you describe something, such as a vacation or a garden, you create a picture with words for your readers. You use details to make the picture specific and real (*We ate **delicious** lobster on our vacation; My aunt has an **exotic, colorful** garden*). Most writers think of the senses—sight, touch, hearing, taste, and smell—to help them describe. If you are careful about choosing just the right descriptive words, your readers will see exactly what you want them to see.

A **descriptive paragraph** is a group of sentences that primarily describes. It can be technical, such as a job description or a lab report. A descriptive paragraph can also tell how you feel about something, such as moving to the United States or starting at a new school. In all good descriptive paragraphs, your readers are able to picture the situation easily in their minds.

Like any paragraph, a descriptive paragraph has a topic sentence with a controlling idea, a body with supporting sentences, and a concluding sentence (see Unit 1, page 2).

Sources: Reading and Analyzing Sample Paragraphs

As you did in Unit 1, in this section you will read two paragraphs that are related in some way. You will study the structure of these paragraphs, understand their meanings, and eventually combine the two ideas to form your own paragraph.

Riding the Train to New York City

PREREADING DISCUSSION QUESTIONS

1. *Have you ever traveled by train or subway? If so, how often? For what purpose?*

2. *How did that experience make you feel? What did you see? Hear? Smell? Taste?*

READING AND ANSWERING QUESTIONS

Read the paragraph that describes a first train ride. Then answer the questions.

SOURCE
1

perspective: view, outlook

trench coat: a belted raincoat in a military style with straps on the shoulders

billboards: advertisement signs in public places

booming: deep and powerful sound

tunnel: an underground passage

RIDING THE TRAIN TO NEW YORK CITY

I saw the world from a new **perspective** when I rode a train for the first time. My friend and I waited in the railway station with people going home from work. We must have looked like students with our jeans and backpacks. I smelled perfume and cigars in the crowd as they walked by us to board the train into the city. People were fairly polite when they stepped up to board the train into the city, with no pushing or shoving. I noticed that most people were carrying briefcases and wore tan **trench coats** with suits underneath. After we found empty seats, we put our backpacks on the metal shelf above us and sat down. The seats felt surprisingly soft and roomy, and we enjoyed relaxing in them. Through the window, we watched small **billboards** speed past us that advertised Broadway shows, designer clothes, and cigarettes. Then, my friend and I looked around the train car and listened while some businessmen spoke in loud, **booming** voices. They shared jokes and stories about their workday. As the ride went on, some passengers fell asleep or read newspapers, while others got on and off at stations. Finally, the train came out of the **tunnel,** and we saw fewer trees and more people and buildings on these streets than in our hometown. This first train ride was certainly nothing like our bus rides home from school.

POSTREADING DISCUSSION QUESTIONS

1. *What is the topic sentence of this paragraph? Write it here. Circle the topic, and underline the controlling idea.*

   _____

   _____

2. *Reread the body of the paragraph, and look for descriptive words. Circle words that express the sense of* sight, *underline the examples of* sound, *draw a box around* smell *words and write an X above examples of touch.*

3. *Descriptions are often organized in order of time when one thing happens after another. Look for some words that show the passage of time, and write them here.*

   _____

   _____

   _____

4. *Underline the concluding sentence. Can you find some important ideas that are the same or similar in both the topic sentence and the concluding sentence? Write some of them here.*

   _____

   _____

   _____

5. *TOEFL Practice*

   *Where would you insert this sentence in the paragraph? (Make a * in the paragraph.)*

   When we heard the conductor shout, "Hoboken, end of the line!" we moved jerkily down the aisle of the moving train with the rest of the crowd to get to the end of the train car.

Taking the "D" Train

PREREADING DISCUSSION QUESTION

Work with a partner. Take turns describing the experience of doing something for the first time. Ask each other questions about your experience, such as the following:

► What was the first-time experience?

► When did it happen?

► How did you feel about it?

► Were there any especially memorable sights or sounds?

EXERCISE 2

READING AND ANSWERING QUESTIONS

Read the paragraph about the New York City subway. Then answer the questions.

SOURCE 2

TAKING THE "D" TRAIN

The first time I rode a New York City subway train, I was surprised at how unpleasant and uncomfortable it was. My friend and I needed to ride the subway across town to get to a concert. The hot underground station smelled bad and was crowded with people. They pushed each other to get close to the yellow line that was painted on the cement floor close to the tracks. When the train pulled in, I was swept into a crowd of people that pushed toward the opening doors. As another mass of people poured off the train, several impatient individuals **darted** into openings in the flow of **exiting** passengers. By the time my friend and I stepped in, the entire car was packed with people, and there were no empty seats. Like the other standing passengers, we held onto the metal bars and handles overhead to keep our balance. The ride was mostly silent except for the wheels **screeching** on the tracks when the train went around curves. Then, at one point, the lights went out for about ten seconds. My friend and I were finally able to sit on the hard, **molded** plastic seats after enough people got off. Next, the loudspeaker made an announcement that we could not hear well or understand. When we looked out the windows at the station signs, we saw that we had arrived at our stop, and we got off as quickly as we could. Nowadays I avoid unpleasant subway trains and take a taxi.

darted: moved suddenly or rapidly

exiting: leaving

screeching: making a high-pitched, harsh sound, like metal on metal

molded: shaped in a certain way

POSTREADING DISCUSSION QUESTIONS

1. *Are Source 1 and Source 2 about the same topic? If so, what is the topic?*

   _____

   _____

2. *What is the topic sentence of Source 2? Write it here. Circle the topic, and underline the controlling idea.*

   _____

   _____

   _____

3. *What words are used to describe the senses (sight, sound, smell, etc.) that you use to understand the meaning of the paragraph? Write the words here.*

   _____

   _____

   _____

4. *What is the concluding sentence of this paragraph? Write it here.*

   _____

   _____

   _____

   What idea is the same in the topic sentence as in the concluding sentence? Write it here.

   _____

   _____

   _____

Organization in Descriptive Writing

Descriptive writing can be organized by using **time** or **space.** Both Source 1 and Source 2 are organized by **time,** with most events happening one after the other. When you organize your descriptive paragraph using space order, you describe where each person, place, or thing is located in relation to the others. Words such as *in front of, next to,* and *over* show this kind of organization.

EXERCISE

3

SPACE ORDER IN DESCRIPTIVE WRITING

Fill in the blanks with words from the chart. Reorganize the paragraph into space order, or in relation to things in the paragraph. Though some words and phrases may work in more than one blank, use each one only once.

in front of	beneath	across from	at the top of
below	behind	next to	over

When my friend and I stepped in, the car was packed with people and there were no empty seats. We looked **(1)** _____ our heads and, like the other standing passengers, we held onto the metal bars and handles to keep our balance. **(2)** _____ the wall, above the passengers' heads, we saw advertisements for computer training courses and radio stations. **(3)** _____ the signs were windows, but it was too dark to see anything passing by. Besides, the passengers' heads **(4)** _____ us blocked our view of the ads. Bits of newspaper, candy wrappers, and empty cigarette boxes were strewn **(5)** _____ the passengers' feet. **(6)** _____ the doors, **(7)** _____ the passenger seats, were two young women who talked constantly to a man **(8)** _____ them.

Transition Expressions

Remember that writers use transition expressions to connect sentences and ideas. Transition expressions also help to show how a paragraph is organized and help it flow smoothly. In descriptive writing, the transition words often show time order, or how events are organized in a sequence, moving from one idea to the next in time.

Before you continue working in this section, reread both Source 1 and Source 2. Circle all of the transition expressions that you think show the passage of time during the train rides.

Unit 2 Transition Expressions: *when, as, while,* and *after*

When

Function: Shows that two things are happening at the same time, or one right after the other.

Use: *When* introduces a dependent clause, so a subject and a verb must follow.

(continued)

(continued)

Punctuation Note: *When* is a subordinating conjunction. Subordinating conjunctions join a main clause and a subordinate clause to form one sentence. If the *when* clause comes at the beginning of a sentence, it is followed by a comma.

Example: *When* John called, I was eating.

If the *when* clause comes at the end of a sentence, no comma is necessary.

Example: I was eating *when* John called.

Practice: Find a sentence in Source 1 that has a *when* clause at the end of the sentence. Write it here.

_____

Find a sentence in Source 2 that has a *when* clause at the beginning of the sentence. Write it here.

_____

As

Function: Shows that two things are happening at the same time.

Use: *As* introduces a dependent clause, so a subject and a verb must follow.

Punctuation Note: Like *when*, the transition word *as* can be used as a subordinating conjunction. When the *as* clause comes at the beginning of a sentence, it is followed by a comma.

Example: <u>As</u> we entered the theater, the play began.

When the *as* clause comes at the end of a sentence, no comma is necessary.

Example: The play began <u>as</u> we entered the theater.

Practice: Find sentences in both Source 1 and Source 2 that use *as* to mean *at the same time that.* Write them here.

Source 1: _____

Source 2: _____

While

Function: Shows that two things are happening at the same time. Unlike *as, while* means that both events began and ended at about the same time.

Use: *While* introduces a dependent clause, so a subject and a verb must follow.

(continued)

(continued)

Punctuation Note: *While* is also used as a subordinating conjunction. When the *while* clause comes at the beginning of a sentence, it is followed by a comma.

Example: While I listened, he talked.

When the *while* clause comes at the end of a sentence, no comma is necessary.

Example: He talked while I listened.

Practice: Find a sentence in Source 1 that contains *while*. Write it here.

_____

After

Function: Shows a time that follows another time.

Use: Like the other transition expressions, *after* is used as a subordinating conjunction. *After* introduces a dependent clause, so a subject and a verb must follow.

Punctuation Note: When the *after* clause comes at the beginning of a sentence, it is followed by a comma.

Example: *After* she ate dinner, she went to a movie.

When the *after* clause comes the end of a sentence, no comma is necessary.

Example: She went to a movie *after* she ate dinner.

Practice: Find a sentence in Source 1 that has an *after* clause at the beginning of the sentence. Write it here.

_____

EXERCISE

WORKING WITH TRANSITION EXPRESSIONS

Fill in the blanks with when, while, as, *or* after. *More than one choice may be correct. Add correct punctuation where necessary.*

1. _____ I was sitting down in my seat, I noticed

   that I had dropped my ticket on the floor.

(continued)

(continued)

2. I folded my newspaper and put it in my briefcase _____
    I finished reading the article.

3. The train schedule will change _____ the holiday
    season has ended.

4. _____ he was waiting, he wrote a list of things he
    needed to buy at the store.

5. _____ the train pulled into the station, the waiting
    passengers got up from the bench.

6. She woke up from a short nap _____ she heard the
    conductor call her stop.

7. She answered the call _____ her cell phone rang.

8. _____ she talked on her cell phone, the other passengers
    looked on in disapproval.

9. The lights came on in the train _____ it got dark
    outside.

10. _____ the train moved along on the tracks, none
    of the passengers said a word.

Paraphrasing, Summarizing, and Synthesizing

In academic writing, you will often have to write information based on something you have read. Therefore, it is important to learn how to **paraphrase** (use different language to say the same thing), **summarize** (express the same idea in a smaller number of words), and **synthesize** (combine information from two or more sources) to answer a specific question of interest. (See Unit 1, pages 14–25, for more about these skills.)

Paraphrasing: An Important Composition Skill

Paraphrasing is putting other people's ideas in your own words. In academic writing, you will often be asked to restate someone else's ideas in your own words.

Here is a paraphrase of a sentence in Source 1.

Original:

We must have looked like students with our jeans and backpacks.

Paraphrase:

Our informal clothes and backpacks made it clear that we were students.

(For more about paraphrasing and a list of verbs to use when you introduce information from a source, see Unit 1, pages 14–15.)

EXERCISE

4

SOURCE 1
Page 42

PARAPHRASING: MULTIPLE CHOICE

*Read the original sentence from Source 1 and Source 2. Then read the three possible paraphrases. Mark one **B** (BEST), one **TS** (TOO SIMILAR), and one **D** (DIFFERENT—or wrong—information).*

1. People were fairly polite when they stepped up to board the train to the city, with no pushing or shoving.

   _____ A. People were mostly polite as they stepped up to board the train to the city, without pushing or shoving.

   _____ B. For the most part, the passengers were courteous to each other as they got on the train.

   _____ C. Not one person used rude language while boarding the train.

SOURCE 2
Page 44

2. Next, the loudspeaker made an announcement that we could not hear well or understand.

   _____ A. Then the public address system announced something that was almost incomprehensible.

   _____ B. After that, an announcement was made by the loudspeaker that we could neither hear well nor understand clearly.

   _____ C. We could not hear because of all the noise in the subway system.

EXERCISE

5

PARAPHRASING PRACTICE

Read these original sentences from Sources 1 and 2. Circle what you consider to be the most important ideas. Then in number 1, choose the best paraphrase for the original sentence. In number 2, write your own paraphrase of the sentence. (See Unit 1, pages 14–15, for more information on paraphrasing.)

1. After we found empty seats, we put our backpacks on the metal shelf above us and then sat down.

    _____ A. We sat down after we found some seats and then put our backpacks away.

    _____ B. After we found empty seats, we put our backpacks on the shelf above us and sat down.

    _____ C. We followed the lead of the passengers with briefcases and stashed our backpacks on the shelf above our seats before sitting down.

2. As another mass of people poured off the train, several impatient individuals darted into openings in the flow of exiting passengers.

Your paraphrase:

_____

_____

_____

_____

Summarizing

Remember that a summary is a shortened version, in your own words, of someone else's ideas. See Unit 1, pages 18–21, for more information about summarizing.

EXERCISE

6

SUMMARIZING: FINDING THE MOST IMPORTANT IDEAS

Reread Source 2 on page 44. Then make a list of up to four important facts or ideas. Use your paraphrasing skills, and do not copy word for word. You must write information in your own words. It is not necessary to use complete sentences.

1. _____

_____

_____

2. _____

_____

_____

3. _____

_____

_____

4. _____

_____

_____

SUMMARIZING: PUTTING IT IN YOUR OWN WORDS

Using your ideas from Exercise 6, write two to five sentences that summarize the original message of Source 2. Reread the section on Summarizing in Unit 1 (pages 18–21) before you begin.

_____

_____

_____

_____

_____

_____

_____

_____

_____

_____

_____

Synthesizing

As you learned in Unit 1, to synthesize is to take information from different sources and blend the information smoothly into one paragraph. Synthesis is important when you read two sources on the same topic and need to combine ideas from both of those sources into your academic writing. See Unit 1, page 22, for more information about synthesizing.

EXERCISE

8

STEPS IN SYNTHESIZING

Follow these steps to organize information from Sources 1 and 2 for synthesizing in the chart below.

1. *Find the main ideas from the topic sentences in Sources 1 and 2. Write them in boxes 2 and 8.*

2. *Write two unique supporting details from Source 1 in boxes 1 and 3.*

3. *Write two unique supporting details from Source 2 in boxes 7 and 9.*

4. *Write three supporting details from both sources in boxes 4, 5, and 6.*

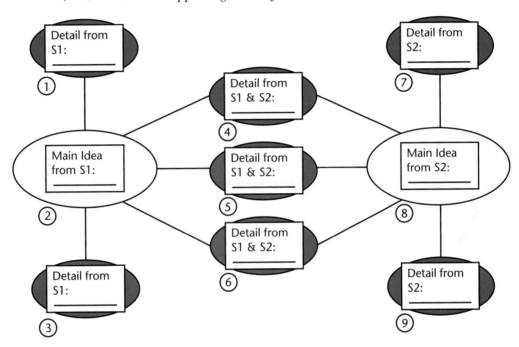

Detail from S1: _____ (1)

Detail from S2: _____ (7)

Detail from S1 & S2: _____ (4)

Main Idea from S1: _____ (2)

Detail from S1 & S2: _____ (5)

Main Idea from S2: _____ (8)

Detail from S1 & S2: _____ (6)

Detail from S1: _____ (3)

Detail from S2: _____ (9)

EXERCISE

9

SYNTHESIZING: EXAM QUESTION PRACTICE

Imagine that you are a student in a journalism class. In a paragraph of four to eight sentences, write your answer to the following question. Synthesize the information from Sources 1 and 2 about train rides.

JOURNALISM EXAM QUESTION:

Many people commute from the suburbs to the city, first taking a commuter train, then a subway train within the city. In one paragraph, describe both the train ride in Source 1 and the subway ride in Source 2 to tell the complete story of getting into New York City by train from the suburbs of New Jersey.

Follow these steps to synthesize the ideas that you organized in Exercise 8.

1. *Begin by combining the information in boxes 2 and 8 into one topic sentence.*

2. *Write supporting sentences that include details in boxes 4, 5, and 6.*

3. *End with a concluding sentence that restates the main ideas of your topic sentence.*

_____

_____

_____

_____

_____

_____

_____

_____

_____

_____

_____

_____

_____

_____

_____

_____

The Writing Process: Practice Writing Descriptive Paragraphs

Objectives	In Part B, you will:
Prewriting:	learn the technique of freewriting to generate writing ideas
Planning:	use a flowchart to organize and sequence ideas
First draft:	write a descriptive paragraph
Partner feedback form:	review classmates' paragraphs and analyze feedback
Second draft:	use peer feedback to write a second draft
Editing:	
Grammar Focus:	practice using prepositions of location, direction, and time
Sentence Check:	identify sentence parts, including subject, verb, object, adjective, and prepositional phrase
Mechanics:	learn how and when to use commas with prepositional phrases
Final draft:	complete the final draft of a descriptive paragraph

The Writing Process: Writing Assignment

Your assignment is to write an original paragraph of five to ten sentences describing your first day of school when you were a child. Use your imagination if you don't remember exactly. Follow the steps in the writing process in this section.

Prewriting: Freewriting

Freewriting is a kind of brainstorming in which you write about a focused idea for several minutes without stopping. As you freewrite, you often think of related ideas about the topic, so the freewriting itself helps you to create more ideas for the first draft of your paragraph.

A Three-Minute Freewriting Exercise

Get Started

To get started freewriting, think about your first day of school as a child. What do you remember? What were the sights and sounds that impressed you? What did you do on that day? What did you feel? On a separate sheet of paper, begin writing whatever comes into your mind as you think about these questions. Do not worry about correct grammar or even about writing full sentences. Write for three minutes without stopping so that your ideas flow.

Identify Related Ideas

When you have finished, look over what you wrote. Choose one idea that you would like to use for your topic sentence, and circle it. Next, underline a few details that you will use to support this topic sentence, and write *S* (for *supporting*) above each one. Cross out any ideas that do not relate to your topic sentence. Below is a model of this freewriting exercise.

FREEWRITING MODEL

My First Day of School

It was 1967 and my family had just moved back to the East Coast—
had been living with my grandparents—was only temporary—two months
I walked to school with my mother (held hands) down tree-lined streets—
wore a brown dress that I loved—all little girls wore dresses to school—
I was happy and excited walking to school and most of the day.
We practiced writing our names
I liked my teacher, Mrs. Packard—she played a piano in the
classroom and taught us songs
~~The second week of school was easier than the first week.~~
The boys played with large wooden blocks and trucks—I wanted to
play with them, but the girls had to play with the dolls so I was not happy.
I was happy to see my mother at the end of the day and walk home.

Planning: Sequencing Ideas with a Flowchart

The next step is to plan how to organize your ideas. You will also
generate more ideas in this step. For your descriptive paragraph, choose
either time order or space order, both described below, to organize your ideas.
Then use one of the flowcharts to sequence the ideas in your freewriting.

Time-Ordered Description

To show the passage of time in description, writers often use words such
as *first, then,* and *next.*

Examples:

Next, the loudspeaker made an announcement that we
could not hear well or understand.

Finally, the train came out of the tunnel, and we saw
fewer trees and more people and buildings on these
streets than in our hometown.

If you choose time order for your descriptive paragraph, organize your
ideas from the previous exercise (and any other ideas that come to you) using
the following flowchart. You do not have to write complete sentences.

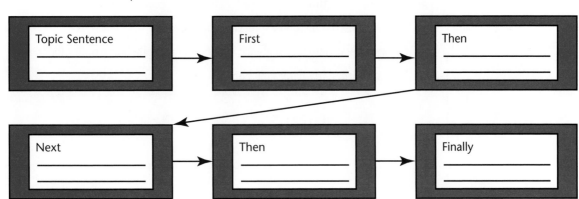

Space-Ordered Description

A different way to organize ideas for a description is according to where things are physically in a space. Think about how your ideas are related to each other in the space you describe. Look at the words in Exercise 3 on page 46 for ideas. If you choose space order for your descriptive paragraph, write your ideas from your freewriting (and any other ideas that come to you) in the following flowchart. You do not have to write complete sentences.

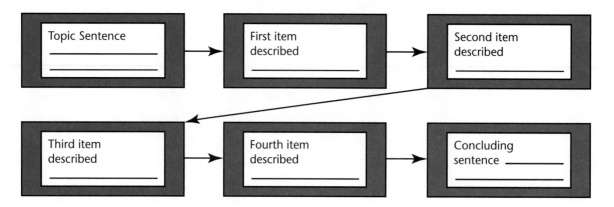

First Draft

You are now ready to write the first draft of your paragraph. Use your flowchart as a guide, and write complete sentences. Remember to think of the senses—sight, touch, hearing, taste, and smell—as you describe your first day of school. Remember to use the transition expressions *when, as, while,* and *after* if possible.

First Draft Checklist

When you finish your paragraph, use this checklist to review your writing.

First Draft Checklist

1. Do I have a topic sentence that contains a clear topic and controlling idea?

2. Are all the sentences about the topic?

3. Are my descriptions vivid and do they include some of the senses—sight, touch, hearing, taste, and smell?

4. Is my use of time or space order correct? (Check the flowchart.)

5. Have I used transition expressions correctly?

6. Does my concluding sentence sum up the paragraph or express feelings?

7. Did I format my paragraph correctly?

Peer Review

Exchange papers with another student. Read your partner's paper, and answer the questions on Partner Feedback Form: Unit 2, page 195. Discuss your partner's reactions to your paragraph. Make notes about any parts you need to change in your second draft.

Second Draft

Second draft revising should include more than grammar, punctuation, and spelling corrections. You should also be checking the topic sentence, the supporting details, the concluding sentence, and the overall completeness and clarity of your paragraph. Now carefully revise your paragraph, using feedback from your partner and your own ideas for revising.

Second Draft Checklist I

1. Is my topic sentence easy for the reader to understand?

2. Does the topic sentence give an idea of what the paragraph is about?

3. Are all the sentences about this topic? Is there any sentence that does not belong here?

4. Is there any sentence that seems out of order?

5. How many transition expressions are there? (Underline them.)

6. Have I considered all my partner's comments and suggestions?

Editing: Grammar and Mechanics

Now that your paragraph has taken shape and the content is clear, it is time to edit for grammar and mechanics.

Grammar Focus: Prepositional Phrases

A prepositional phrase consists of a preposition and its object, for example, *at the station. At* is the preposition, and *station* is the object. Prepositional phrases often help describe location, direction, and time.

Examples:

Location: She lived *on Avenue B.*

Direction: Reginald walked *across the campus.*

Time: Class starts *at 8:30.*

EXERCISE

10

GRAMMAR: IDENTIFYING PREPOSITIONAL PHRASES OF LOCATION, TIME AND DIRECTION

*Write an **L** (location), **D** (direction), or **T** (time) in front of each of the following prepositions or prepositional phrases. The first one has been done for you.*

1. ___D___ onto the train

2. _____ outside the station building

3. _____ down the aisle

4. _____ in the afternoon

5. _____ around the car

6. _____ on the metal shelf

7. _____ after work

8. _____ on the station platform

9. _____ through the window

10. _____ above us

EXERCISE

11

GRAMMAR: PREPOSITIONAL PHRASES IN DESCRIPTION

Add prepositional phrases to the sentences below, which describe walking into a classroom for the first time. Make sure your sentences make sense. The first one is done for you.

1. I found the classroom easily because there was a sign *above the door* _____.

2. Once in the room, I looked _____ and saw that there were no other students _____ .

3. Finally, a young woman came _____ and sat down _____ .

4. Next, I noticed that _____ were written the words, BUY YOUR TEXTBOOKS _____ .

5. I walked _____ and then sat down _____ .

6. To be ready, I took my pen and notebook _____ and placed them _____ .

EXERCISE 12

DESCRIPTION IN TIME ORDER WITH PREPOSITIONS

Now organize the sentences you completed in Exercise 11 into a short paragraph. Use time order in a logical sequence.

_____

_____

_____

_____

_____

_____

_____

_____

_____

_____

Sentence Check: Parts of a Sentence: Subject, Verb, Object, Adjective, and Prepositional Phrase

In English, a sentence must have a subject and a verb. It can also have an object, an adjective, an adverb, and a prepositional phrase.

S V O adv. Adj. PP

Example:

Nick serves food quickly in the Greek delicatessen.

▶ The **subject** is a noun or pronoun that does the action or experiences the state. The subject is often a noun phrase and can include an adjective or a prepositional phrase. In the example sentence, the subject is *Nick*.

▶ The **verb** is the action word. The verb phrase may include adverbs and adverbial phrases. In the example sentence, the verb is *serves*.

▶ The **object** receives the action. In the example sentence, the object is *food*.

▶ The **adverb** describes the verb and answers the question "How does Nick serve food?" In the example sentence, the adverb is *quickly*.

▶ An **adjective** describes a noun. In the example sentence, the adjective is *Greek* (referring to what kind of delicatessen).

▶ A **prepositional phrase** is a preposition and its object (noun or pronoun) and can serve many functions. In the example sentence, the prepositional phrase is *in the Greek delicatessen.*

EXERCISE 13

IDENTIFYING SUBJECTS, VERBS AND OBJECTS

Read each sentence. Circle the subject, underline the verb, and draw a box around the object. The first one has been done for you.

1. (Hirumi) bought a new jacket.

2. Insun and Shellie took the bus to the shopping center.

3. They found a nice sweater on the sale rack.

4. Shopping bores their boyfriends.

5. After shopping, they love to eat dinner at the Chinese restaurant.

6. No one has an appetite as big as Insun's.

7. She ate five egg rolls.

8. Shellie opened her fortune cookie.

9. Before they got up, they left a tip.

10. This restaurant takes no reservations.

EXERCISE 14

PARTS OF A SENTENCE: OBJECT, ADJECTIVE, AND PREPOSITIONAL PHRASE

*Decide whether the underlined words in the sentences below are objects, adjectives, or prepositional phrases. Write **O** (object), **A** (adjective), or **PP** (prepositional phrase) in front of each sentence. The first one has been done for you.*

1. _A_ George became <u>angry</u> when the train was late.

2. _____ Loud planes are flying <u>over our heads</u>.

3. _____ Fatima always wears <u>a long scarf</u> over her head in the convertible.

4. _____ Kevin canoes <u>up the river</u> every weekend in the summer.

5. _____ Luisa takes <u>very long trips</u> for her job.

6. _____ The music coming from the boat sounds <u>wild and fun</u>.

7. _____ The price of the flight was <u>unusual</u> for that time of the year.

8. _____ She said she is going <u>around the corner</u> on her motorcycle.

9. _____ We will leave the house <u>in the afternoon</u> on our scooters.

10. _____ Everyone took <u>a train schedule</u> for the ride home.

Mechanics: Commas with Prepositional Phrases

Writers usually put a comma after a prepositional phrase when it comes at the beginning of a sentence.

Example:

In the room with the copy machine, he found his car keys.

You do not need to use a comma if the prepositional phrase is at the end of the sentence.

Example:

He found his car keys in the room with the copy machine.

EXERCISE

15

COMMAS WITH PREPOSITIONAL PHRASES

Read each sentence, and add commas where needed.

1. I will always keep in touch with you.
2. She likes to order pizza after the movies.
3. After some careful thought they decided to take a trip during winter break.
4. During the past semester Hank's grades improved.
5. Taylor always sets the alarm before he goes to sleep at night.
6. There was a presidential election in November 2000.
7. On a trip to Latin America he wrote letters home.
8. He tore off his sweatshirt as soon as he got into his room.
9. Before tasting her food Vanessa smelled it carefully.
10. They often watch television news in the evening.

Return to Your Second Draft

Now look at your second draft again, and check these items. Make corrections where necessary.

Second Draft Checklist II

1. Are any prepositional phrases of location, direction, and time punctuated correctly?
2. Does each of your sentences have a subject and a verb?
3. Are your subjects, verbs, and objects in the correct order?
4. Check carefully for run-on sentences, comma splices, and fragments. (See Appendix 2, Appendix 3, and Appendix 4 for more information on these three sentence problems.)
5. Have you used the transitions *when, as, while,* and *after*? If so, are they correctly punctuated?

Final Draft

Carefully revise your paragraph, using all of the feedback you have received: partner feedback form, instructor comments, and self-evaluation. In addition, try reading your paragraph aloud. This can help you find awkward-sounding sentences and errors in punctuation. When you have finished, neatly type your final draft.

Additional Writing Assignments from the Academic Disciplines

Beginning with the prewriting activity on page 56, go through the process of writing another descriptive paragraph. Choose a topic from the following list.

SUBJECT	*WRITING TASK*
Business	Write a job description for a person that you need to hire.
Culture	Write a description of a holiday or tradition that is meaningful to you.
Science	Write a description of the subject of an experiment, such as an animal, plant, or cell, based on your observation of it.
Media studies	Write a description of a celebrity who is currently famous.
Health care	Write a description of the symptoms of a person who is ill.

Blueprints for

PROCESS PARAGRAPHS

Blueprints for Process Paragraphs

Objectives	In Part A, you will:
Analysis:	identify the key features of process paragraphs
Transitions:	learn to use *first, next, finally,* and *then*
Practice:	paraphrase, summarize, and synthesize information

What Is a Process Paragraph?

When you explain how to do something (such as how to assemble a bicycle) or how something happens (such as how a glacier moves), you use a process to talk about the steps or events. A **process paragraph** is a group of sentences that tells this sequence.

A process paragraph consists of a series of connected steps. The steps must be logical and are often chronological in order. You can use time words and transition expressions to make the sequence of events or actions clear. Process writing is especially important when you want to explain the steps necessary to complete a task. Process paragraphs usually demonstrate how to do something.

You are probably familiar with a common kind of process writing: a recipe. For the result to be a success, the steps in a recipe must be clear, in the correct order, and concise. In academic settings, process writing is commonly used in science classes and labs, information technology courses, and many other disciplines.

Sources: Reading and Analyzing Sample Paragraphs

The two paragraphs in this section are related in some way. You will study the structure of these paragraphs, understand their meanings, and eventually combine the two ideas to form your own paragraph.

Polygraph Testing

PREREADING DISCUSSION QUESTIONS

1. *Do you ever lie? How do you know if a person is lying? Can you tell by the way the person looks or acts?*

2. *Do you know what a polygraph test is and how it works?*

READING AND ANSWERING QUESTIONS

Read the paragraph that describes the process of a polygraph test. Then answer the questions. As you read, pay attention to the process that occurs.

physiological: relating to the physical processes of an organism

device: a machine

respiratory: breathing

pulse: rhythmic beats caused by the contractions of the heart

tip: the point or end of an object

electrode: a device used to transmit electric current

preceding: previous, former

POLYGRAPH TESTING

Many people know the terms *polygraph* and *lie detector test*, but many are not familiar with how this test actually works. The test uses a process that analyzes the **physiological** reactions in a person's body while he or she answers questions. First, a **device** called a pneumograph is attached to a person's chest to record breathing patterns. Any abnormalities in **respiratory** patterns are recorded during an official interview. Next, a machine similar to those used in doctors' offices is attached to the person's upper arm to measure blood pressure. During this part of the polygraph test, the **pulse** and changes in blood pressure and heartbeat are recorded. Finally, skin responses are used as part of the lie detection examination. Usually, the **tips** of a person's fingers are attached to **electrodes.** An abnormal amount of sweating is an indicator that the person may be lying. After the **preceding** steps have been followed, polygraph experts analyze the results. From the data, the experts may conclude that the person is telling the truth, or they may decide that the person is probably lying.

POSTREADING DISCUSSION QUESTIONS

1. What is the topic sentence of this paragraph?

    _____

    _____

2. Reread the body of the paragraph and look for the three parts of the polygraph test process. What are they?

    _____

    _____

3. Find five transition expressions in the paragraph that show time or the passage of time. Write them here.

    _____

    _____

4. In process paragraphs, the topic sentence and the concluding sentence usually have a different relationship than in the other kinds of paragraphs you have studied. The concluding sentence is often about the result of the process and does not necessarily reflect the topic sentence. Reread and underline the concluding sentence. What is the final result of the polygraph process?

    _____

    _____

5. *TOEFL Practice*

    Where would you insert this sentence in the paragraph? (Make a *5 in the paragraph between the two sentences.)

    This portion of the polygraph test that analyzes blood pressure is often shown in movies and television shows.

6. *TOEFL Practice*

    Where would you insert this sentence in the paragraph? (Make a *6 in the paragraph between the two sentences.)

    These electrodes record the amount of perspiration that a person develops while he or she is answering questions.

DNA the Easy Way

PREREADING DISCUSSION QUESTIONS

1. What is DNA testing?
2. Do you think DNA testing should be used in court as evidence about crimes?
3. Is DNA testing common in your native country? Why or why not?

EXERCISE

2

READING AND ANSWERING QUESTIONS

Read the paragraph about DNA testing. Then answer the questions.

IMPORTANT NOTE:

DNA (deoxyribonucleic acid) testing is a scientific method for establishing people's identities. It can be used to identify criminals, eliminate the possibility of someone's guilt, or determine the biological likelihood of a parent-child relationship. As you read, pay attention to the process of performing a DNA test.

cheek: the fleshy part of the face between the mouth and the ear

swab: an absorbent stick

extract: withdraw

probe: an instrument used to explore an area

strand: a length twisted together like a rope

reliable: trustworthy, sure

DNA THE EASY WAY

Believe it or not, the process of completing a DNA test is not very difficult. First of all, human cells must be collected. The cells can be collected from a person's **cheek** using a **swab.** The next step is to send this cell sample to a laboratory, where scientists **extract** the DNA from the swab and create many samples from it. Then the samples are put into a gel mixture and are subjected to an electric current. A DNA **probe** can then be used, which attaches itself to the sample. Each person produces a unique location of DNA attachment, and this is how the identification works. Ultimately, scientists develop the film of this unique DNA **strand.** This type of DNA test becomes more **reliable** as more probes are used to test the strand. DNA testing has become very popular, so it is now available on the Internet. Ordinary people can now order in-home DNA tests and get their results in just a few days.

POSTREADING DISCUSSION QUESTIONS

1. *What is the topic sentence of this paragraph?*

   _____

2. *The paragraph tells how simple DNA testing is done. Fill in the missing information about the test (the steps) from the paragraph.*

   Step 1: Collect the sample

   Step 2: _____

   Step 3: Extract the DNA

   Step 4: Create many samples

   Step 5: _____

   Step 6: Add electric current

   Step 7: _____

   Step 8: Analyze the probe's location

   Step 9: _____

3. *In "Polygraph Testing" on page 67, you located transition words that show a time relationship. Two of them were* first *and* finally. *What two transition words or phrases in "DNA the Easy Way" can you find that have similar meanings?*

   first = _____

   finally = _____

4. *Reread the last two sentences in the paragraph. What surprising information is given in these sentences? With what idea do they conclude the paragraph?*

   _____

   _____

5. *TOEFL Practice*

   Where would you insert this sentence in the paragraph? (Make a *5 in the paragraph between the two sentences.)

   This electric current separates the smaller DNA samples from the larger ones.

6. *TOEFL Practice*

   Where would you insert this sentence in the paragraph? (Make a *6 in the paragraph between the two sentences.)

   The key to using DNA testing is analyzing where this probe attaches itself.

Transition Expressions

In process writing, transition words and expressions are needed specifically to make the steps in the process clear. These transition expressions help the ideas or steps in the process flow from one to the next so that the reader can follow them logically and easily. Without the appropriate transition expressions, the paragraph is just a list of steps.

Unit 3 Transition Expressions: *first, next, then,* **and** *finally*

First

> **Function:** signals the first step
>
> **Use:** *First* is an adverb and is usually followed by a subject and a verb. However, *first* can also come in the middle or at the end of the sentence. In many cases, the imperative verb form (command form) comes after the word *first* to give directions.
>
> *Example:* First, apply for the job.

> **Punctuation Note:** When *first* comes at the beginning of a sentence, it is followed by a comma.
>
> *Example:* First, Emilio applied for the job.

When *first* comes in the middle or at the end of a sentence, no comma is necessary

> *Examples:* Emilio first applied for the job.
>
> Emilio applied for the job first.

(continued)

(continued)

Practice: Find the sentence in Source 1 that contains the word *first*. Write it here.

_____

CAREFUL! **Firstly, secondly,** and **thirdly** are commonly used in British English but not in Standard American English.

Next

Function: signals the step after the previous step or action

Use: *Next* is an adverb. It can come at the beginning or at the end of a sentence. Just as you can with *first*, you can follow *next* with a subject and a verb or use the imperative form.

Example: <u>Next</u>, schedule an interview.

Punctuation Note: When *next* comes at the beginning of a sentence, it is followed by a comma.

Example: <u>Next</u>, Emilio scheduled an interview.

When *next* comes at the end of a sentence, no comma is necessary.

Example: Emilio went for an interview <u>next</u>.

Practice: Find the sentence in Source 1 that contains the word *next*. Write it here.

_____

Then

Function: signals the step after the previous step or action

Use: *Then* is an adverb. The most common position for *then* is at the beginning of a sentence, followed by the subject and verb.

Example: <u>Then</u> Emilio waited for an offer.

A more formal position of *then* is directly after the subject and before the verb.

Example: Emilio <u>then</u> waited for an offer.

Punctuation Note: No comma is necessary with *then*.

Finally

Function: signals the last step in the process or action

Use: *Finally* is an adverb. It is used at the beginning of a sentence to signal the last, or final, step of a process.

Example: <u>Finally</u>, send the company a thank-you note for the interview.

(continued)

(continued)

Finally can appear in the middle and at the end of the sentence. In these cases, it means "at last" and does not signal the last step in a process.

Example: Emilio <u>finally</u> made an appointment for an interview.

Punctuation Note: When *finally* comes at the beginning of a sentence, it is followed by a comma.

Practice: Find the sentence in Source 1 that contains the word *finally.* Write it here.

_____

Example: *First,* weigh the patient on the scale. *Next,* take the patient's temperature. *Then* take his or her blood pressure. *Finally* (NOT *in conclusion*), tell the patient to wait for the doctor.

CAREFUL!   Do **not** confuse the transition words **finally** and **in conclusion**. The adverb **finally** is not used to signal the end of the paragraph. It is used to signal the final step (reason, example) in a sequence.

EXERCISE

WORKING WITH TRANSITION EXPRESSIONS

Read the paragraph. Fill in each blank with first, next, then, *or* finally. *Some transitions may fit into more than one blank. Add correct punctuation where necessary.*

It is easy to make a telephone call if you follow these simple directions. To make the call, _____ you must know the telephone number you are dialing. _____ pick up the phone and listen for the dial tone. _____ you can start dialing the telephone number. If the person answers the phone, begin speaking. If an answering machine clicks on, wait for the beep and record your message. _____ hang up the phone when you have finished your call.

Paraphrasing, Summarizing, and Synthesizing

Before you continue, review these important skills in Unit 1, pages 14–25.

Paraphrasing: An Important Composition Skill

(For information about paraphrasing and a list of verbs to use when you introduce information from a source, see Unit 1, pages 14–15.)

EXERCISE

3

PARAPHRASING PRACTICE

*Read the original sentence. Then read the three possible paraphrases. Mark one **B** (BEST), one **TS** (TOO SIMILAR), and one **D** (DIFFERENT—or wrong—information).*

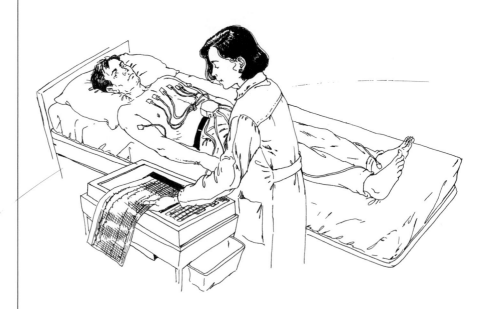

SOURCE
1
Page 67

1. Next, a machine similar to those used in doctors' offices is attached to the person's upper arm to measure blood pressure.

_____ A. The next step is to attach a machine to the person's arm to measure blood pressure. This machine is much like the one used in doctors' offices.

_____ B. Next, an expensive piece of equipment is used to measure the blood pressure of the person. This part of the polygraph usually makes the person very nervous.

_____ C. After that, a machine similar to those used in physicians' offices is connected to the person's arm to measure blood pressure.

SOURCE **2** Page 69

2. The next step is to send this cell sample to a laboratory, where scientists extract the DNA from the swab and create many samples from it.

_____ A. Sample DNA is then sent to a laboratory, where the DNA is extracted from the swab and many samples can be created from it.

_____ B. The laboratory portion of the test is the most important, and scientists cannot make any mistakes during this process.

_____ C. After that, the DNA sample is given to laboratory scientists. They are able to create numerous samples of this DNA by drawing it out of the swab.

EXERCISE

4

PARAPHRASING: PRACTICE

Read these original sentences from Sources 1 and 2. Circle what you consider to be the most important ideas. Then in number 1, choose the best paraphrase for the original sentence. In number 2, write your own paraphrase of the sentence. (See Unit 1, pages 14–15, for more information on paraphrasing.)

SOURCE **1** Page 67

1. This portion of the polygraph test that analyzes blood pressure is often shown in movies and television shows.

_____ A. This painful part of the polygraph test, which is the most reliable, usually tells the most information about a person's truthfulness.

_____ B. Commonly seen in movies and TV shows, this part of the polygraph exam measures the blood pressure of the person.

_____ C. People may recognize this portion of the polygraph test because it is commonly seen in films.

SOURCE **2** Page 69

2. Each person produces a unique location of DNA attachment, and this is how the identification works.

Your paraphrase: _____

Number of words: _____

Summarizing

(For information about and guidelines for summarizing, see Unit 1, pages 18–21.)

EXERCISE 5

SUMMARIZING: PUTTING IT IN YOUR OWN WORDS

Source 2, "DNA the Easy Way," contains 164 words. Summarize the paragraph in approximately 50 words. Follow the steps presented in Unit 1, pages 18–21, to write your summary. Note that the summary begins with "according to" in the topic sentence to show where the information came from. Use correct paragraph format (see Unit 1, pages 18–21). You should write no more than five sentences in your summary.

According to "DNA the Easy Way," _____

_____

_____

_____

_____

_____

_____

_____

Synthesizing

To review the steps in synthesizing, see Unit 1, page 22, and Unit 2, page 53.

EXERCISE 6

SYNTHESIZING: EXAM QUESTION PRACTICE

Imagine that you are a student in a criminology class. In a paragraph of four to eight sentences, write your answer to the following exam question. Synthesize the information from Sources 1 and 2 about polygraph and DNA tests. Remember that you must write information in your own words.

HUMAN BIOLOGY EXAM QUESTION:

On the basis of the information you now have about polygraph testing and DNA testing, write a paragraph explaining the importance of body fluids (perspiration, saliva, etc.) in these two scientific methods.

_____

_____

_____

_____

_____

_____

_____

_____

_____

_____

_____

_____

_____

_____

_____

_____

_____

_____

_____

_____

_____

_____

PART B

The Writing Process: Practice Writing Process Paragraphs

Objectives	In Part B, you will:
Prewriting:	use a questionnaire to generate ideas for writing
Planning	write chronological steps
First draft:	write a process paragraph
Partner feedback form:	review classmates' paragraphs and analyze feedback
Second draft:	use peer feedback to write a second draft
Editing:	
Grammar Focus:	practice subject-verb agreement
Sentence Check:	identify compound sentences patterns with *and, but, so,* and *or*
Mechanics:	learn correct paragraph title format
Final draft:	complete the final draft of a process paragraph

The Writing Process: Writing Assignment

Your assignment is to write an original paragraph of five to ten sentences about a profession you are interested in. Write the process of how to become a professional in that field.

Prewriting: Answering Questions

Asking and answering questions can help a writer generate ideas for writing. When writers think about possible topics, they often ask questions such as "What do I know how to do well?" or "What specific details do readers need to know about this step in the process?" Asking questions helps to generate details that can make the writing clearer.

Interest Questionnaire

One way to help generate questions and answers is to use a questionnaire. To get started with this freewriting strategy, answer the questions in the following questionnaire. Your answers will help you see what your interests are.

Interest Questionnaire

1. My favorite subject in school was/is: _____

   _____

2. I like working with:

   numbers

   people

   schedules

   my hands

   abstract problems

3. I like to work/study:

   alone

   with others

   indoors

   outdoors

4. I am interested in the field of

   business

   the arts

   economics

   natural science

   engineering

   humanities

   political science

   other: _____

5. My favorite hobbies are: _____

   _____

6. I enjoy talking (discussing) with others.   YES   NO

   If you answered YES, write down the topics that you truly enjoy talking about with other people.

   _____

   _____

   _____

Narrowing the Topic

In groups of three or four, compare answers from your questionnaire. As a group, discuss what kinds of job fit well with your areas of interest. Then on your own, choose *one* subject area that you are particularly interested in and find the answers to these questions about it:

▶ Do you need a high school degree to perform this job?

▶ Do you need a specific college degree to perform this job?

▶ Do you need to pass a standard exam before beginning this job?

▶ Do you need practical training before beginning this job?

IMPORTANT NOTE:

If you need help finding the answers, try searching the
Internet or asking your instructor or a librarian.

Planning: Chronological Steps

Now that you have chosen the profession you will write about, the next activity is to organize the steps to becoming a professional in that field. Complete this outline with steps in chronological order to help with the organization   of your paragraph.

How to become a/an _____
The steps involved in this process:

Step 1: _____

_____

Step 2: _____

_____

Step 3: _____

_____

Step 4: _____

_____

Step 5: _____

IMPORTANT NOTE:

Your paragraph may have more or fewer than five steps.

_____

Conclusion: _____

_____

First Draft

You are now ready to write the first draft of your paragraph. As a guideline, use the chronological steps that you just outlined. Remember to use the transition expressions *first, next, then,* and *finally.*

First Draft Checklist

When you finish your paragraph, use this checklist to review your writing.

First Draft Checklist

1. Do I have a topic sentence that contains a clear topic and controlling idea?

2. Are all the sentences about the topic?

3. Are all the steps in the process in logical order?

4. Have I used transition words correctly?

5. Does my concluding sentence sum up the paragraph or express feelings?

6. Did I format my paragraph correctly?

Peer Review

Exchange papers with another student. Read your partner's paper, and answer the questions on Peer Feedback Form: Unit 3, page 197. Discuss your partner's reactions to your paragraph. Make notes about any parts you need to change in your second draft.

Second Draft

Second draft revising should include more than grammar, punctuation, and spelling corrections. You should also be checking the topic sentence, the supporting details, the concluding sentence, and the overall completeness and clarity of your paragraph. Now carefully revise your paragraph, using feedback from your partner and your own ideas for revising.

Second Draft Checklist I

1. Is my topic sentence easy for the reader to understand?

2. Does the topic sentence give an idea of what the paragraph is about?

3. Are all the sentences about the topic? Is there any sentence that does not belong here?

4. Are all the steps in the process present?

5 Is there any sentence that seems out of order?

6. Did I use enough transition expressions to show the sequence of steps?

7. Does my concluding sentence give a positive result of the previous steps?

8. Have I considered all my partner's comments and suggestions?

Editing: Grammar and Mechanics

Reviewing and practicing the following grammatical points will help you self-edit your paragraph for common grammatical mistakes.

Grammar Focus: Subject-Verb Agreement

One challenge in writing English sentences is to make sure the subject and the verb are in grammatical agreement. The main rule is that the subject and the verb must agree in person and in number. This means that singular subjects must take the singular form of the verb and plural subjects must take the plural form of the verb.

Examples:

Singular subject/singular verb:

<u>She</u> <u>parks</u> her car on that street every night.

Plural subject/singular verb:

Many <u>people</u> <u>take</u> that exam.

CAREFUL! The singular form of the verb ends in **s**, while the plural form does not. This is the case for many regular verbs.

Some Troublesome Singulars

All of the following pronouns are singular, even though some of them might sound plural. When you use these pronouns in sentences, remember to make the verb singular.

somebody	nobody	anybody	everybody
somebody	nobody	anybody	everybody
someone	no one	anyone	everyone
something	nothing	anything	everything

Examples:

<u>Everyone</u> in the class <u>has</u> [not *have*] a dictionary.

<u>Anything</u> <u>is</u> [not *are*] possible!

CAREFUL! Sometimes the subject and the verb in a sentence do not occur next to each other. Descriptive words, clauses, or phrases can come between the subject and the verb. To check for correct subject-verb agreement, you first have to locate the subject and the verb.

Examples:

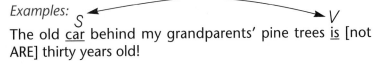

The old <u>car</u> behind my grandparents' pine trees <u>is</u> [not ARE] thirty years old!

The phrase *behind my grandparents' pine trees* is extra information and should not be in agreement with the verb *is*.

GRAMMAR: CHECKING FOR SUBJECT-VERB AGREEMENT

*Read each sentence. If it contains an error in subject-verb agreement, write an **E** (error) on the line and correct the error. If the sentence is correct, write a **C** (correct) on the line.*

1. _____ If you want to study more effectively, you should follow some basic steps.

2. _____ The first step is to practice organization.

3. _____ It is very important to write down assignments, tests, and study times on a calendar.

4. _____ If everything are organized, it is easier to find and review the information.

5. _____ Another important thing to do are find a suitable study area.

6. _____ Library cubicles is often quiet places to read and study.

7. _____ After finding a good study area, you need to concentrate on only one particular assignment.

8. _____ Many times you have a hard time with this because you has not trained your mind to focus on only one thing.

9. _____ Anyone is capable of improving study skills!

10. _____ If you follow the preceding steps, studying will surely be an easier task.

EXERCISE

8

GRAMMAR: CHANGING SUBJECTS AND VERBS TO AGREE

Follow the instructions in parentheses and change the subject in each sentence. Then change the verb to agree with the subject, and write the correct sentence on the line. The first one has been done for you.

SOURCE 1
Page 67

1. Many people know the terms *polygraph* and *lie detector test,* but many are not familiar with how this test actually works. (Change *this test* to *these tests.*)

   Many people know the terms polygraph and lie detector

   test, but many are not familiar with how these tests

   actually work.

2. Any abnormalities in respiratory patterns are recorded during the official interview. (Change *abnormalities* to *abnormality.*)

   _____

   _____

3. After the preceding steps have been followed, polygraph experts analyze the results. (Change *polygraph* experts to *a polygraph expert.*)

   _____

   _____

SOURCE 2
Page 69

4. Each person produces a unique location of DNA attachment, and this is how the identification works. (Change *Each Person* to *All people.*)

   _____

   _____

5. Then the samples are put into a gel mixture and are subjected to an electric current. (Change *samples* to *sample.* Be careful because you will have to make more than one singular/plural change in the sentence.)

   _____

   _____

6. Believe it or not, the process of completing a DNA test is not very difficult. (Change *DNA test* to *DNA tests.* Be careful because this one is different.)

   _____

   _____

Sentence Check: Compound Sentence Patterns with *and, but, so,* and *or*

In English, there are many kinds of sentence patterns. You may be most familiar with simple sentences, which have one subject and one verb. Another sentence pattern is called a **compound sentence,** which is made up of two simple sentences combined. The two sentences are joined by a conjunction, such as *and, but, so,* and *or.* Writers often combine the information in two related simple sentences to make a longer sentence.

Example:

The instructor was not feeling well, *so* she went home.

CAREFUL! When you use a conjunction between two simple sentences, be sure to put a comma (,) before the conjunction.

The Four Most Common Conjunctions

Using examples from the two sources, study the four most common conjunctions in compound sentences.

1. *but:* The conjunction *but* shows contrast.

SOURCE
1
Page 67

Many people know the terms polygraph *and* lie detector test, *but many are not familiar with how this test actually works.*

This compound sentence is made up of two simple sentences that have been combined by using the conjunction *but:*

Sentence 1: Many people know the terms *polygraph* and *lie detector test.*

Sentence 2: Many are not familiar with how this test actually works.

These sentences contrast with each other because the second part of the statement shows an opposition to the first. It is different from what is expected.

Here are two more examples of contrast in compound sentences joined by *but*:

I live in a house, but my brother lives in an apartment.

Lorna wanted to go to the party, but her car would not start.

2. *and*: The conjunction *and* connects additional information.

SOURCE
2
Page 69

Each person produces a unique location of DNA attachment, and this is how the identification works.

This compound sentence is made up of two simple sentences that have been combined by using the conjunction *and*:

Sentence 1: Each person produces a unique location of DNA attachment.

Sentence 2: This is how the identification works.

The second sentence gives more information, usually about the same topic. Because the information in both sentences is closely connected, use the conjunction *and* to make a compound sentence.

Here are two more examples of adding information in compound sentences joined by *and*:

I studied for the final exam, and I went to sleep at midnight.

Italy is in Southern Europe, and it is a peninsula.

3. *so*: The conjunction *so* shows the result of the first action or sentence.

SOURCE
2
Page 69

DNA testing has become very popular, so it is now available on the Internet.

This compound sentence is made up of two simple sentences that have been combined by using the conjunction *or*:

Sentence 1: DNA testing has become very popular.

Sentence 2: It is now available on the Internet.

These sentences show the result. Usually, the clause following the conjunction *so* is a logical effect or result of the original information.
Here are two more examples of showing result in compound sentences joined by *so*:

We had some extra cash, so we decided to eat out.

The thunderstorm was severe, so the county closed all the schools.

4. *or*: The conjunction *or* shows the option (choice) of either the first part of the sentence or the second part of the sentence.

SOURCE
1
Page 67

From the data, the experts may conclude that the person is telling the truth, or they may decide that the person is most likely lying.

This sentence is two sentences that have been combined using the connector *so*:

Sentence 1: From the data, the experts may conclude that the person is telling the truth.

Sentence 2: They may decide that the person is most likely lying.

These sentences show option. One or both situations are possible.
Here are some other examples with *or*:

I might study sociology, or I might major in economics.

Henry can go home alone, or he can go to dinner with some friends.

EXERCISE

9

GRAMMAR: CREATING COMPOUND SENTENCES

Read each pair of simple sentences. Rewrite them as a compound sentence using the conjunction in parentheses. Remember to use a comma before the conjunction.

1. Sentence 1: The police officers demanded a lie detector test. (so)
   Sentence 2: The suspect agreed to take it.

   _____

   _____

2. Sentence 1: The suspect sat down in the investigation chair. (and)
   Sentence 2: The lie detector test began.

   _____

   _____

3. Sentence 1: The suspect was very nervous. (but)
   Sentence 2: He answered all the questions.

   _____

   _____

4. Sentence 1: The investigator told him to relax. (or)
   Sentence 2: The results would not be valid.

   _____

   _____

5. Sentence 1: The suspect understood the process. (but)
   Sentence 2: He was uncomfortable during this time.

   _____

   _____

6. Sentence 1: The suspect became even more nervous. (so)
   Sentence 2: All his answers seemed like lies.

   _____

   _____

EXERCISE
10

GRAMMAR: COMPLETING COMPOUND SENTENCES

Use your imagination to fill in the blanks and make compound sentences.

1. The suspect was put in prison, but _____

_____

2. He called his lawyer, and _____

_____

3. The prisoner wanted a new trial, or _____

_____

4. His lawyer believed in his innocence, so _____

_____

5. The lawyer requested a DNA test, but _____

_____

6. The test was finally agreed to, and _____

_____

7. The prisoner could take the test in prison, or _____

_____

8. The DNA test showed that the prisoner was innocent, so

_____

_____

Mechanics: Paragraph Title Format

The title of your work is the first thing that a reader sees, so you should know the rules for writing a concise and grammatically correct title.

Rules for Creating Titles

1. Titles should represent the main idea of the writing.

2. Titles are usually phrases or fragments; they are *not* complete sentences.

3. Titles do not require periods at the end.

4. The first letter of the first word of a title is *always* capitalized.

5. Only the *important* words in titles are capitalized. Do not capitalize prepositions or articles (unless they are the first word in the title).

6. Titles are not written in all capital letters.

EXERCISE

11

ANALYZING TITLES

Read each title, and give the number of the rule that it does not follow. Then write the title correctly.

1. MY MOST TERRIBLE JOB (rule # _____)

   Correct title: _____

   _____

2. I love my job very much (rule # _____)

   Correct title: _____

   _____

3. becoming an Engineer (rule # _____)

   Correct title: _____

   _____

4. My Paragraph (rule # _____)

   Correct title: _____

   _____

5. My First Job. (rule # _____)

   Correct title: _____

   _____

6. The Best Job Of My Life (rule # _____)

   Correct title: _____

   _____

Return to Your Second Draft

Now look at your second draft again and check these items. Make corrections where necessary.

Second Draft Checklist II

1. Do all of your sentences have correct subject-verb agreement?
2. Do any compound sentences include the correct conjunctions?
3. Are the compound sentences punctuated correctly?
4. Did you include a title for your paragraph? If not, add one now.
5. Make other corrections where necessary.

Final Draft

Carefully revise your paragraph using all of the feedback you have received: partner feedback form, instructor comments, and self-evaluation. In addition, try reading your paragraph aloud. This can help you find awkward-sounding sentences and errors in punctuation. When you have finished, neatly type your final draft.

Additional Writing Assignments from the Academic Disciplines

Beginning with the prewriting activity on page 79, go through the steps of writing another process paragraph. Choose a topic from the following list:

SUBJECT	*WRITING TASK*
Technology	Write a process paragraph about how to program a piece of equipment, such as a microwave or a VCR.
Science	Choose a natural phenomenon such as lightning, a tornado, or a geyser. Explain how it is formed.
Sociology	Choose a cultural event from your country, such as marriage or an engagement. Explain the steps involved in this event.
Practical	Explain the process of getting a driver's license, passport, or other official document.

UNIT

4

Blueprints for

DEFINITION PARAGRAPHS

Blueprints for Definition Paragraphs

Objectives	In Part A, you will:
Analysis:	identify the key features of definition paragraphs
Transitions:	learn to use *this, according to,* and *in fact*
Practice:	paraphrase, summarize, and synthesize information

What Is a Definition Paragraph?

def•i•ni•tion (dĕfə-nĭsh´ən) *n.* **1.** [C] A statement that explains the meaning of sthg., such as a word or phrase, as in a dictionary entry. **2.** [U] The act of making (sthg.) clear and distinct: *a definition of one's purposes.*

When you write a paragraph that consists of an extended definition of a term or concept, you are writing a **definition paragraph.** However, when you write a definition paragraph, you give much more than a simple definition. You also give examples of the term and explain it for readers as thoroughly and clearly as possible.

In academic settings, you may have to write extended definitions of important words or phrases. Sometimes you are asked to identify or define a term. In an exam in a business class, for example, the instructor might ask you to define *macroeconomics.* Your answer might be a definition paragraph. In this paragraph, you would give an opening topic sentence and then a sentence that defines the term *Macroeconomics.* You might follow this with an example of macroeconomics.

Another example of writing a definition paragraph might be in a literature course in which you have to write an essay about the symbolism found in a particular poem or short story. Of course, most of the essay would be about the symbolism in the story, but one paragraph in that essay could be an extended definition of *symbolism.*

Sources: Reading and Analyzing
Sample Paragraphs

In this section, you will read two paragraphs that are related in some way. You will study the structure of these paragraphs, understand their meanings, and eventually combine the two ideas to form your own paragraph.

SOURCE 1

HIV

PREREADING DISCUSSION QUESTIONS

1. *What is HIV?*

2. *How can people know with certainty whether or not they have HIV?*

3. *Do you agree or disagree with the following statement? "Most people who have HIV know they have this disease." Explain your answer.*

4. *How does HIV harm a person?*

5. *About how many people in the United States do you think have HIV? About how many worldwide?*

EXERCISE 1

READING AND ANSWERING QUESTIONS

Twenty-five years ago, almost no one knew what HIV was. Unfortunately, this term is now a household word. Read the paragraph about HIV. Then answer the questions.

acronym: a series of capital letters that stands for a longer term and can be spoken like a word (example: TOEFL = Test of English as a Foreign Language)

semen: the white secretion of the male reproductive organs that contains sperm

vaginal fluids: liquids secreted in the vagina (the passage leading to the uterus in female mammals)

break down: to stop working

spread: to move into many places

symptoms: signs (especially of disease or illness)

aware: to know about (used with verb BE)

obvious: clear, easy to see

HIV

HIV is the **acronym** for the human immunodeficiency virus that eventually leads to the disease known as AIDS. HIV is transmitted among people through body fluids, including blood, **semen,** breast milk, and **vaginal fluids.** When this virus attacks a person, it causes the immune system to **break down.** This weakening of the body's natural defense system allows certain deadly diseases to attack and **spread.** Some people develop **symptoms** shortly after infection. According to the Centers for Disease Control (CDC), as many as 34.3 million people may be infected with this virus. As many as one in three individuals with HIV is not **aware** that he or she is infected. The spread of the virus greatly concerns doctors because there are no **obvious** signs that a person has HIV. In fact, the only certain way of determining whether a person is carrying HIV is through a blood test.

POSTREADING DISCUSSION QUESTIONS

1. What is the topic sentence of this paragraph?

_____

_____

2. The paragraph discusses four fluids that carry HIV. What are they?

_____

_____

*3. Underline the three places where the word **this** occurs. What does this refer to in each case?*

_____

_____

4. TOEFL Practice

Where would you insert this sentence in the paragraph? (Make a *4 in the paragraph between the two sentences.)

Others may not show any signs for more than ten years.

5. TOEFL Practice

Where would you insert this sentence in the paragraph? (Make a *5 in the paragraph between the two sentences.)

The T4 cells, which are an important part of the immune system, are common targets of the virus, which then weakens the body.

AIDS

PREREADING DISCUSSION QUESTIONS

1. *What is AIDS?*

2. *What do you know about the number of AIDS cases? What do you know about the number of AIDS deaths?*

3. *Do you think everyone should be required to take an AIDS test? Should only certain people take the test? Why or why not?*

EXERCISE

READING AND ANSWERING QUESTIONS

Read the paragraph about AIDS. Then answer the questions.

IMPORTANT NOTE:

AIDS has become a leading killer in many parts of the world. As you read, focus on the extended definition of what AIDS is.

The AIDS quilt remembers those who have died of AIDS. For more information, go to http://www.aidsquilt.org/

cripples: limits or restricts severely

ravage: attack

stages: levels, steps, or part of something

tangible: concrete, easy to see

fatigue: tired

tumor: a noninflammatory growth that is independent of the area where it is growing and that serves no bodily function

while: although

AIDS

AIDS, or acquired immune deficiency syndrome, is a severe disease that **cripples** the body's immune system so severely that other diseases are able to **ravage** the body. The term *AIDS* applies to the most advanced **stages** of HIV infection. More specifically, the Centers for Disease Controls says that a person has AIDS when his or her T4 cell count drops to less than 200. **Tangible** signs that indicate that an individual might have this illness include coughing and shortness of breath, serious weight loss, extreme **fatigue**, brain **tumors,** various cancers, and other health problems. All of these effects are serious and, without proper treatment, can kill the person. **While** there are no drugs to cure AIDS, there are medicines to prevent or treat some of the related problems. With more than 775,000 cases of AIDS reported in the United States since 1981 and more than 18.8 million cases worldwide, AIDS continues to be a serious threat to the world's population.

POSTREADING DISCUSSION QUESTIONS

1. What is the topic sentence of this paragraph?

_____

2. The paragraph presents signs that tell people that they have AIDS. Look at the following list. Fill in the missing information from the paragraph.

General: AIDS is the advanced stage of _____*.*

Specific: AIDS is present when a person's T4 count _____

_____

Symptoms: _____

_____

_____

_____

*3. One way to introduce examples in a definition paragraph is to use the verb **include**, for example, "Examples of this **include** x, y, and z." Write the sentence that contains the verb **include** here.*

_____

_____

*4. Find the word **these** in the paragraph. What does the word **these** refer to?*

_____

_____

5. Reread the last sentence of this definition paragraph. What do you think its purpose is?

_____

_____

6. TOEFL Practice

Where would you insert this sentence in the paragraph? (Make a *6 in the paragraph between the two sentences.)

By comparison, a healthy person's T4 count is 1,000 or more.

Transition Expressions

In writing definitions, transition words and expressions are helpful to give extra information to the reader. A transition can emphasize the information presented. Transition words and expressions help the reader understand the flow of ideas from one to the next.

Unit 4 Transition Expressions: *this (+ noun), according to, and in fact*

this

Function: indicates a reference to something that was just said

Use: *This* is an adjective that specifies which particular thing is being talked about.

Example: This test is the hardest one we have taken all semester.

Grammar Note: *This* may occur alone or with a noun. It may occur in the subject position or in the object position in a sentence.

Examples:

With a noun, subject position: After months of drought, the eastern part of Texas received more than six inches of rain. While *this* wet weather was welcome to farmers in the area, the heavy rain also caused flooding in some parts of the region.

Alone; subject position: Many doctors' offices and health clinics offer testing for HIV. *This* can be done anonymously if the person does not want his or her real name connected to any test results.

With a noun, object position (object of the preposition of*):* The prime minister claimed yesterday that his predecessor stole more than twenty million dollars from the government in the early 1990s. Political analysts are debating the credibility of *this* accusation.

Alone; object position (object of the verb believe*):* Some scientists believe that AIDS may have existed for many years before the current epidemic. They believe *this* because of recent medical evidence that shows that AIDS occurred in certain animals for some time before it showed up in humans.

Practice: Find a sentence in Source 1 that contains the word *this*. Write it here.

_____

_____

(continued)

(continued)

Find a sentence in Source 2 that contains the word *this*. Write it here.

_____

_____

according to

Function: introduces specific facts taken from a source such as a dictionary, a newspaper article, or an expert in the field

Use: *According to* is used to cite (give credit to) a person or a source that has stated this information.

Grammar Note: *According to* is always followed by a noun, noun phrase (according to *what* or *whom*?), or pronoun.

Example: According to health experts, people should get at least 45 minutes of exercise four times per week in order to stay healthy.

Punctuation Note: When *according to* is part of an introductory phrase, the phrase is followed by a comma.

Practice: Find the sentence in Source 1 that contains the phrase *according to*. Write it here.

_____

_____

in fact

Function: introduces a specific example of the previous, more general statement

Use: *In fact* is often used when a writer wants to be emphatic and make an additional, related point.

Grammar Note: *In fact* almost always occurs at the beginning of a sentence. It is followed by a subject and a verb.

Example: Mushrooms are a good food to eat if you are on a diet. In fact, a whole cup of mushrooms contains fewer than 15 calories.

Punctuation Note: Always put a comma after *in fact*.

Practice: Find the sentence in Source 1 that contains the phrase *in fact*. Write it here.

_____

_____

(continued)

Working with Transition Expressions

*Read the paragraph. Fill in each blank with **this (+ noun)**, **according to**, or **in fact.** Some transitions may fit into more than one blank. Add correct punctuation where necessary.*

A new kind of ticket for air travel in the last decade is the electronic ticket. _____ new kind of ticket, which has revolutionized check-in at the airport, is commonly referred to as an e-ticket. An e-ticket is a paperless ticket for air travel that is sent to the traveler via e-mail. Many travelers using an e-ticket for the first time are surprised that there is no printed ticket. _____ a traveler can purchase the ticket, get a confirmation number, and check in at the airport without any kind of printed paper from the airline. For obvious reasons, _____ paperless method of ticketing is extremely popular. Many travelers are unsure of e-tickets at first. _____ most airline analysts, however, the use of airline tickets is growing, and they may eventually replace traditional paper tickets one day.

Paraphrasing, Summarizing, and Synthesizing

Before you continue, review these important skills in Unit 1, pages 14–25.

Paraphrasing: An Important Composition Skill

(For information about paraphrasing and a list of verbs to use when you introduce information from a source, see Unit 1, pages 14–15.)

EXERCISE 3

PARAPHRASING: MULTIPLE CHOICE

*Read the original sentence. Then read the three possible paraphrases. Mark one **B** (BEST), one **TS** (TOO SIMILAR), and one **D** (DIFFERENT—or wrong—information).*

SOURCE **1**
Page 95

1. As many as one in three individuals with HIV is not aware that he or she is infected. (33 words)

_____ A. About one-third of people who are infected with HIV may not know that they have this disease.

_____ B. One in three people with HIV is not aware that he or she has HIV.

_____ C. About two in three people with HIV know with certainty that they have this serious disease.

SOURCE **2**
Page 96

2. While there are no drugs to cure AIDS, there are medicines to prevent or treat some of the related problems. (*20 words*)

_____ A. There is no cure for AIDS itself, but certain medicines can treat or avoid some of the health problems associated with AIDS.

_____ B. The medicines that are useful for treating AIDS offer a cure.

_____ C. Although there are no drugs to cure AIDS, there are some medicines to prevent or treat several of the related problems.

EXERCISE 4

PARAPHRASING PRACTICE

Read these original sentences from Sources 1 and 2. Circle what you consider to be the most important ideas. Then in number 1, choose the best paraphrase for the original sentence. In number 2, write your own paraphrase of the sentence. (See Unit 1, pages 14–15, for more information on paraphrasing.)

Page 95

1. The spread of the virus greatly concerns doctors because there are no obvious signs that a person has HIV.

   _____ A. Many doctors are worried because they may spread HIV to their patients.

   _____ B. The spread of the HIV virus concerns doctors very much because there are no clear signs that an individual has HIV.

   _____ C. Doctors are worried about the spread of HIV because infected people may not know that they have HIV.

Page 96

2. With more than 775,000 cases of AIDS reported in the United States since 1981 and more than 18.8 million cases worldwide, AIDS continues to be a serious threat to the world's population.

   Your paraphrase:

   _____

   _____

Summarizing

(For information about and guidelines for summarizing, see Unit 1, pages 18–21.)

EXERCISE 5

SUMMARIZING: PUTTING IT IN YOUR OWN WORDS

Source 2 about AIDS contains 156 words. Summarize the paragraph in approximately 50 words. Follow the steps presented in Unit 1, pages 18–21, to write your summary. Use correct paragraph format, with a topic sentence (See Unit 1, pages 18–21). You should write no more than five sentences in your summary. Remember that you must write information in your own words.

_____

_____

_____

_____

_____

_____

_____

Synthesizing

To review the steps in synthesizing, see Unit 1, page 22, and Unit 2, page 53.

EXERCISE	SYNTHESIZING: EXAM QUESTION PRACTICE

6

Imagine that you are a student in a health class. In a definition paragraph of four to eight sentences, write your answer to the following exam question. Synthesize the information from Sources 1 and 2 about HIV and AIDS. See Unit 1, page 22, for more information about synthesizing.

HEALTH EXAM QUESTION:

Many people confuse HIV and AIDS, but these two terms actually refer to separate things. On the basis of what you have learned about HIV and AIDS, write a paragraph defining them. In your discussion, include information on symptoms and infection rates.

_____

_____

_____

_____

_____

_____

_____

_____

_____

_____

_____

_____

The Writing Process: Practice Writing Definition Paragraphs

Objectives

In Part B, you will:	

Objectives	In Part B, you will:
Prewriting:	list general nouns and adjective clauses for definitions
Planning:	provide important details
First draft:	write a definition paragraph
Peer review:	review classmates' paragraphs and analyze feedback
Second draft:	use peer feedback to write a second draft
Editing:	
Grammar Focus:	practice correct use of articles *a, an,* and *the*
Sentence Check:	identify adjective clauses (*who/whom, that,* and *which*)
Mechanics:	learn correct punctuation with restrictive and nonrestrictive adjective clauses
Final draft:	complete the final draft of a definition paragraph

The Writing Process: Writing Assignment

Your assignment is to write an original definition paragraph of five to ten sentences about a term related to a subject that you are interested in. For example, if you are interested in computers, you might write about *databases.* If you are interested in business, you might write about *macroeconomics.* If you are interested in politics, you might write about a *theocracy.* In your definition paragraph, be sure to explain the term and then give details and examples.

COMPUTER SCIENCE

economics literature political science

biology

health art anthropology

Prewriting: Listing General Nouns and Adjective Clauses

It goes without saying that the definition of a term is important to your definition paragraph, so you want to use the best possible wording. A useful prewriting technique is to list several general nouns and adjective clauses that define the term. Then you can choose the best general one for your definition.

For example, if the assignment requires a definition of "a good friend," you might produce this list:

A good friend is . . .	*who . . .*
a person	will help you when you have a problem
a companion	will never let you down
a soulmate	will be there for you every time no matter what
a guy	you can depend on in all kinds of circumstances

As you write your definition paragraph, you can choose the definition that best fits your meaning.

Sentence Pattern

When you define a term in your definition paragraph, you will probably write a sentence that follows this pattern:

A ____*the term*____ is a ____*general noun*____ that/who ____*adjective clause that describes or limits the definition*____.

Here are a few examples of this sentence pattern:

A *giraffe* is an *animal* that *has a long neck and very tall legs.*

A *hurricane* is a *tropical storm* that *has extremely high winds and large amounts of rain.*

AIDS is a *disease* that *attacks the human immune system.*

Notice that the example list above about a good friend follows this sentence pattern.

PREWRITING: BRAINSTORMING KEY DEFINITION WORDS IN A LIST

Work with a partner. Come up with at least three general nouns and three adjective clauses for definitions of these words. When you have finished, decide on the best general noun and the best adjective clause. Write your original definition on the line.

1. Define "true love."

   True love is a _____ that _____.

   1. _____   1. _____
   2. _____   2. _____
   3. _____   3. _____

2. Define "a good teacher."

   A good teacher is a _____ who _____.

   1. _____   1. _____
   2. _____   2. _____
   3. _____   3. _____

3. Define "_____." (Choose a word with your partner.)

   _____ is a _____ that/who

   _____.

   1. _____   1. _____
   2. _____   2. _____
   3. _____   3. _____

4. Define "_____." (Choose a word with your partner.)

   _____ is a _____ that/who

   _____.

   1. _____   1. _____
   2. _____   2. _____
   3. _____   3. _____

Planning: Providing Important Details

You have already practiced the first two steps in writing a definition paragraph: (1) choosing a topic and (2) writing a definition with a general noun followed by an adjective clause. This definition is your topic sentence. The next step is to add two or three sentences of examples or related information about the term that you are defining.

Study this outline of Source 2 on page 96:

TOPIC SENTENCE: AIDS, or acquired immune deficiency syndrome, is a severe disease that cripples the body's immune system so severely that other diseases are able to ravage the body.

IMPORTANT INFORMATION:

1. Diagnosis that a person has AIDS
   A. Most advanced stage of HIV = AIDS
   B. CDC says that T4 cell count of less than 200 = AIDS
   C. Certain physical conditions = AIDS
      1. Coughing
      3. Shortness of breath
      4. Serious weight loss
      4. Extreme fatigue
      5. Brain tumors
      6. Various cancers
      7. Other health problems

2. Possibility of cure or treatments

3. Number of cases (worldwide and U.S.)

4. Concluding sentence

Note that the writer begins with a definition of AIDS (topic sentence), gives supporting information that explains more about the disease (body), and ends with a concluding sentence. This is the usual pattern of the three main parts of a paragraph (see Unit 1, page 2).

EXERCISE
8

ORGANIZING: PROVIDE IMPORTANT DETAILS

Follow these guidelines:

► If you have not done so already, choose a topic for your definition paragraph.

► Write a definition (topic sentence) according to the pattern in the prewriting section.

► Decide what important details you will include in your paragraph. Write this information in the following outline.

Term that you are defining: _____

Topic (definition) sentence: _____

_____

Important details: _____

_____

_____

_____

_____

_____

Conclusion: _____

_____

First Draft

Now you are ready to write the first draft of your paragraph. As a guide, use the outline you just created in Exercise 8. Remember to use the transition expressions *this (+ noun)*, *according to*, and *in fact*.

First Draft Checklist

When you finish your paragraph, use this checklist to review your writing.

***

First Draft Checklist

1. Did I include a topic sentence that identifies the term I am defining?

2. Does the topic sentence have a general noun in it?

3. Is there an adjective clause after the general noun (beginning with *that* or *who*)?

4. Are the important details in the supporting sentences related to the topic sentence?

5. Is the information presented in logical order?

6. Did I use transition words correctly?

7. Does my concluding sentence sum up the paragraph?

8. Did I format my paragraph correctly?

Peer Review

Exchange papers with another student. Read your partner's paper and answer the questions on Partner Feedback Form: Unit 4, pages 199–200. Discuss your partner's reactions to your paragraph. Make notes about any parts you need to change in your second draft.

Second Draft

Remember that second draft revising should include more than grammar, punctuation, and spelling corrections. You should also be checking the topic sentence, the supporting details, the concluding sentence, and the overall completeness and clarity of your paragraph. Now carefully revise your paragraph using feedback from your partner and your own ideas for revising.

Second Draft Checklist I

1. Is my topic sentence easy for the reader to understand?

2. Is the topic sentence a definition sentence?

3. Does the topic sentence give a clear idea of what the paragraph is about?

4. Are all the sentences about this topic? Is there any sentence that does not belong here?

5. Is there any sentence that seems out of order?

6. How many transition expressions are there? (Underline them.)

7. Have I considered all my partner's comments and suggestions?

Editing: Grammar and Mechanics

Reviewing and practicing the following grammatical points will help you self-edit your paragraph for common grammatical mistakes.

Grammar Focus: Articles

One of the most difficult areas of English grammar is using the articles *a, an,* and *the*. These three little words cause many problems for writers in English.

There are three common errors that students make with articles: (1) using an article when none is required, (2) not using an article when one is required, and (3) using the wrong article.

ERROR 1:

Using an Article When None Is Required

The most common example of Error 1 is to use *the* when no article is required.

> **RULE:** Do not use the with general ideas or names.

Incorrect: <u>The</u> tennis is the best sport for young children to learn because it involves the body and the mind.

Correct: Tennis is the best sport for young children to learn because it involves the body and the mind.

Incorrect: The most important subject for a young student who is interested in becoming an astronaut is <u>the</u> science.

Correct: The most important subject for a young student who is interested in becoming an astronaut is science.

At other times, a writer might make the mistake of putting *a* or *an* with noncount nouns.

> **RULE:** Do not use *a* or *an* with a noncount noun.

Incorrect: Do you have a change for this dollar? I'd like to make a call.

Correct: Do you have change for this dollar? I'd like to make a call.

ERROR 2:

Not Using an Article When One Is Required

The most common examples of Error 2 are as follows:

▶ Forgetting to use *a* or *an* with a singular count noun (bicycle, fork)

> **RULE:** A singular count noun must have some kind of article [a, an, or the] in front of it.

▶ Forgetting *the* in front of certain geographical names

> **RULE:** Use *the* with bodies of water [except a single lake], mountain ranges [except a single mountain], and countries [and other geographical features] that contain the words *Republic, Kingdom, Union,* or *United* or end in *–s*.

Incorrect: If a student has good dictionary, then she can look up the meaning of unknown word.

Correct: If a student has <u>a</u> good dictionary, then she can look up the meaning of <u>an</u> unknown word.

Incorrect: The cargo shipment was sent from United States to the Malta, which is an island in Mediterranean Sea.

Correct: The cargo shipment was sent from <u>the</u> United States to _____ Malta, which is an island in <u>the</u> Mediterranean Sea.

ERROR 3:

Using the Wrong Article

The most common example of Error 3 is when a writer uses *a* or *an* instead of *the* (or *the* instead of *a* or *an*). This usually happens in referring to something for the second or third time. In this case, it is necessary to use *the*.

> **RULE:** Use *the* when referring to something for the second or additional time.

Incorrect: President Richard Nixon made a decision in the 1970s to increase U.S. dialogue with China. A decision to do this resulted in much better relations between two countries.

Correct: President Richard Nixon made a decision in the 1970s to increase U.S. dialogue with China. <u>The</u> decision to do this resulted in much better relations between <u>the</u> two countries.

| EXERCISE 9 | # GRAMMAR: EDITING FOR ARTICLES I |

Read the sentences in this definition paragraph about accounting. There are five errors with articles: Error 1 (two), Error 2 (two), and Error 3 (one). Correct the errors.

ACCOUNTING

Accounting is the process of systematically collecting, analyzing, and reporting a financial information. Accounting information is used primarily by the management of a company, but it is also demanded by lenders, suppliers, stockholders, potential investors, and the government agencies. Private accountant is employed by a specific organization to operate the accounting system in that particular organization. The public accountant performs these functions for various individuals or firms on fee basis. Most accounting firms include on their staff at least one certified public account (CPA).

From *Business*, Sixth Edition, by Pride, Hughes, & Kapoor. Copyright © 1999 Houghton Mifflin Company. Reprinted with permission.

| EXERCISE 10 | # GRAMMAR: EDITING FOR ARTICLES II |

Read the sentences in this definition paragraph about phonemes. There are five errors with articles: Error 1 (one), Error 2 (two), and Error 3 (two). Correct the errors.

THE SMALLEST UNIT OF SOUND

A phoneme is a smallest unit of sound that affects the meaning of a speech. Changing a phoneme changes the meaning of a spoken word, much as changing a letter in a printed word changes its meaning. Tea has meaning that is different from sea, and sigh is different from sign. While each spoken language consists of thirty to fifty phonemes, English is the average language with about forty phonemes. Printed letters are not always same as phonemes. In English, the letter *a* in *cat* and the letter a in cake, for example, represent different phonemes although they are the same written letter. Though a phoneme is small, it can change the meaning of a person's message.

From D. A. Bernstein, A. Clarke-Stewart, L. A. Penner, E. J. Roy, and C. D. Wickens, *Psychology,* 5th ed. (Boston: Houghton Mifflin, 2000) pp. 274–275.

Sentence Check: Adjective Clauses (*Who/Whom, That*, and *Which*)

In definition paragraphs, an easy way to be more specific when you are identifying an object or a person is to use an adjective clause. (An adjective clause is also called a relative clause. In this book, we use the term *adjective clause.*) An adjective clause describes or identifies a noun. Adjective clauses commonly begin with *who, whom,* or *that* when you refer to a person and *which* or *that* when you refer to a thing.

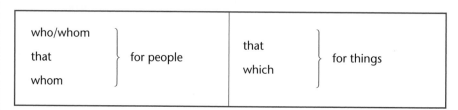

who/whom			that		
that	}	for people		}	for things
whom			which		

In the following examples, some information from the first sentence is included in the second sentence. Notice that the third sentence includes information from both the first and second sentences.

Example A:
1. The book is on the table.
2. The book has a shiny green cover.
3. The book *that has a shiny green cover* is on the table.

Example B:
1. I would like to read the book.
2. The book has a shiny green cover.
3. I would like to read the book *that has a shiny green cover.*

Example C:
1. The book is on the table.
2. I bought the book for my father.
3. The book *that I bought for my father* is on the table.

Example D:
1. The customer left without a receipt.
2. The customer bought the book.
3. The customer *who bought the book* left without a receipt.

An adjective clause can modify two basic parts of a sentence: subject or object. *Who, that,* and *which* can begin adjective clauses in the subject position, while *who, whom, that,* and *which* can begin adjective clauses in the object position.

Adjective Clauses That Modify Subjects: *Who, That,* and *Which*

Remember that a subject is the doer of the action or state of being in a sentence. In the following example, *telephone* is the subject: The telephone is out of order. Suppose we want to add this information: The telephone is on the desk. We can include it in the main sentence as an adjective clause that describes the subject:

The telephone *that is on the desk* is out of order.

Here is another example in which *player* is the subject: The player will get a trophy. Suppose we want to add this information: The player wins the championship match. We can include it in the main sentence as an adjective clause that describes the subject:

The player *who wins the championship match* will get a trophy.

IMPORTANT NOTE:

The word *that* and the rest of the adjective clause describe the subject *telephone*.

IMPORTANT NOTE:

The word *who* and the rest of the adjective clause describe the subject *player*.

Adjective Clauses That Modify Objects: *Who, Whom, That,* and *Which*

Remember that the object of a verb receives the action of that verb.

1. *who* versus *whom*: In adjective clauses in the object position, *whom* is the correct objective form. However, it is common to use *whom* in academic or formal writing and *who* in informal writing and in conversation. (In other words, in informal and conversational English, people avoid using *whom*.)

Academic/formal: In this example, *runner* is the object: Jack is the runner. Suppose we want to add this information: We watched Jack in the race. We can include it in the main sentence as an adjective clause that describes the object:

Jack is the runner *whom we watched in the race.*

Informal/conversation:

Jack is the runner <u>who</u> *we watched in the race.*

2. Optional *who, whom, that,* and *which*: In adjective clauses in the object position, you may omit *who, whom, that,* and *which* at the beginning of the clause in the cases of informal writing and conversation. However, in academic and formal writing, it is best to always include these words.

Academic/formal:

Dr. Talbot is the speaker *whom we invited to the fundraiser.*

Informal/conversation:

Dr. Talbot is the speaker *who we invited to the fundraiser.*

Very informal/conversation:

Dr. Talbot is the speaker *we invited to the fundraiser.*

EXERCISE 11

CREATING ADJECTIVE CLAUSES

Read each pair of sentences. Rewrite them as one sentence using an adjective clause. Then write S (subject) or O (object) on the line to show whether the adjective clause is in the subject or object position.

SOURCE 1
Page 95

1. Sentence 1: HIV is the acronym for the human immunodeficiency virus.

   Sentence 2: The virus eventually leads to the disease known as AIDS.

   _____

   _____

   Position in sentence: _____

SOURCE 2
Page 96

2. Sentence 1: Tangible signs include coughing and shortness of breath, serious weight loss, extreme fatigue, brain tumors, various cancers, and other health problems.

   Sentence 2: These signs indicate that an individual might have this illness.

   _____

   _____

   Position in sentence: _____

3. Sentence 1: HIV is a medical condition.

   Sentence 2. HIV precedes AIDS.

   _____

   _____

   Position in sentence: _____

4. Sentence 1: Doctors are testing potential vaccines.

   Sentence 2: Millions of people could benefit from these vaccines.

   _____

   _____

   Position in sentence: _____

5. Sentence 1: Because of the intricate workings of the AIDS virus, a cure for AIDS is extremely difficult to develop.

   Sentence 2: The cure might deal with both HIV and AIDS.

   _____

   _____

   Position in sentence: _____

6. Sentence 1: The information was inaccurate.

   Sentence 2: We got the information from the web site *www.hiv.net.*

   _____

   _____

   Position in sentence: _____

EXERCISE

12

COMPLETING SENTENCES WITH ADJECTIVE CLAUSES

Make up an adjective clause to complete each sentence.

1. The company's profit was less than the amount _____

   _____

   _____ .

2. Because of the drought conditions, _____

_____, this year's harvest
of corn was not very good.

3. Several members of the committee _____

_____ disagreed with the
chairperson's decision.

4. Charlene was ecstatic when she got the job _____

_____

_____.

5. Voters _____
elected Susana Powers as their representative.

6. Jambalaya is a spicy dish _____

_____.

Mechanics: Punctuation with Restrictive and Nonrestrictive Adjective Clauses

To understand how to use commas with adjective clauses, you need to know about the two types of adjective clauses: restrictive and nonrestrictive.

Restrictive Adjective Clauses

Restrictive adjective clauses contain information that is necessary to understand the meaning of the noun that the clause describes. We say that the adjective clause "restricts" the meaning to what is in the clause. Because the information in this kind of adjective clause is necessary, no commas are used to set it off from the rest of the sentence.

Example:

The *man* <u>who called the police</u> saw the accident.

▶ The noun is *man.*

▶ Ask: *Which man?* If the answer is specific and not just *any* man, a restrictive clause follows.

▶ The restrictive adjective clause is *who called the police.*

▶ Because the clause is restrictive, no commas are used.

Nonrestrictive Adjective Clauses

Nonrestrictive adjective clauses contain information that is *not* necessary to understand the meaning of the noun that the clause describes. We say that the clause "does not restrict" the meaning of the noun because the noun has already been identified or explained sufficiently. This happens especially when the noun is a proper noun (the name of the person or thing) or when there is only one person or thing.

Example:

AIDS, which is a leading killer in Africa, became a household word in the United States in the 1980s.

▶ The noun is *AIDS*.

▶ Ask: *What about AIDS?* If the answer is not necessary to understand AIDS in this context, a nonrestrictive clause follows.

▶ The nonrestrictive adjective clause is *which is a leading killer in Africa.* This is simply additional information, and the sentence makes sense without it (*AIDS became a household word in the United States in the 1980s.*)

▶ Because the clause is nonrestrictive, commas are used to set it off from the rest of the sentence.

EXERCISE

13

COMMAS WITH NONRESTRICTIVE ADJECTIVE CLAUSES

Read the sentences and add commas to the clauses where necessary. Not all sentences need commas.

1. Niels Bohr is a name that is quite well-known in the field of physics.

2. As a young boy, Niels Hendrik David Bohr (1885–1962) lived in the shadow of his younger brother Harald who played on the 1908 Danish Olympic Soccer Team.

3. Niels struggled with writing during his entire life.

4. Despite his genius, the poorest school marks that Bohr received were in composition.

5. His writing was so bad that he is one of the very few people who felt the need to write rough drafts of postcards.

6. Despite these problems with writing, Bohr who was always good at math and science persevered.

7. Bohr's Ph.D. thesis which was actually written by his mother from his own notes received critical acclaim.

8. After receiving his Ph.D. in Denmark, he constructed a quantum model for the hydrogen atom.

9. Even though his model later proved to be incorrect, Bohr remained a central figure in the drive to understand the atom.

10. For the outstanding contributions that Bohr made to the scientific community, Bohr was awarded the Nobel Prize in physics in 1922.

From *Introductory Chemistry* by Steven Zumdahl. Copyright © 2000 Houghton Mifflin Company. Reprinted with permission.

Return to Your Second Draft

Now look at your second draft again and check these items. Make corrections where necessary.

Second Draft Checklist II

1. Did you write any adjective clauses? If so, check whether they are in the subject or the object position. Then make sure the beginning word is correct (*who, whom, that,* or *which*).

2. If you did not use any adjective clauses, add two adjective clauses in your writing now. Good writers use adjective clauses freely to help the reader!

3. Did you remember to use commas in nonrestrictive clauses?

4. Check each article (*a, an, the*) and make sure it is correct.

5. Did you forget any articles?

6. Did you include a title for your paragraph? If not, add one now.

7. Work with a partner on the Partner Feedback Form again. Make corrections where necessary.

Final Draft

Carefully revise your paragraph using all of the feedback you have received: partner feedback review, instructor comments, and self-evaluation. In addition, try reading your paragraph aloud. This can help you find awkward-sounding sentences and errors in punctuation. When you have finished, neatly type your final draft.

Additional Writing Assignments from the Academic Disciplines

Beginning with the prewriting activity on page 106, go through the writing process and write another definition paragraph. Choose a topic from the following list

SUBJECT	WRITING TASK
Culture/anthropology	Write about *xenophobia*.
Chemistry	Write about *trace elements*.
Health care	Write about *hepatitis C*.
U.S. history	Write about *carpetbaggers*.
Architecture	Write about *Doric architecture*.
Practical	Write about an international food that most people would not be familiar with.

5

Blueprints for

COMPARISON/CONTRAST PARAGRAPHS

PART A

Blueprints for Comparison/Contrast Paragraphs

Objectives	In Part A, you will:
Analysis:	identify the key features of comparison/contrast paragraphs
Transitions:	learn to use *like, the same . . . as, in contrast,* and *whereas*
Practice:	paraphrase, summarize, and synthesize information

What Is a Comparison/Contrast Paragraph?

In a **comparison/contrast paragraph,** you work with two people, two ideas, or two things. For example, you might write about mountain bicycles and racing bicycles. To **compare** them, you explore both their similarities and differences. A comparison then can include the things that are the same and the things that are different. If you **contrast** the two kinds of bicycles, you include only the differences between them.

Comparing and contrasting are strategies that help to explain and analyze people, ideas, or things. You can use the skills of comparing and contrasting in many aspects of your lives. For example, as consumers, you might compare cars to decide which one to buy. In the business world, you might want to compare two stocks or other investment opportunities. In an academic setting, you might need to decide which of two theories or ideas you agree with. In academic courses, you will often be asked to write comparison/ contrast responses to essay questions. This means that you need to include both the similarities and the differences in your answer.

CAREFUL! Writing a comparison/contrast paragraph is not always as easy as it sounds. Subjects that are too similar (football and rugby) or too different (apples and hamburgers) will not lead to a coherent paragraph. There should be an underlying similarity or difference in your topics. A good example is comparing the agility of a football player and that of a ballerina. On the surface, the two occupations seem completely different, but they both require agility.

Sources: Reading and Analyzing Sample Paragraphs

In this section, you will read two paragraphs that are related in some way. You will study the structure of these paragraphs, understand their meanings, and eventually combine the two ideas to form your own paragraph.

SOURCE
1

The Internet and Intranets

PREREADING DISCUSSION QUESTIONS

1. *Do you know the difference between the Internet and an intranet?*

2. *Which features of these two kinds of networks are the same? Which are different?*

EXERCISE

1

READING AND ANSWERING QUESTIONS

Read the paragraph that compares the Internet to an intranet. Then answer the questions.

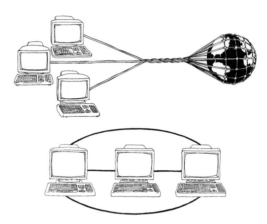

SOURCE
1

network: a system of computers interconnected in order to share information

data: information in a form that can be processed by a computer

hypertext: a computer-based system that enables a user to access particular locations in web pages or other electronic documents by clicking on links within specific web pages or documents

protocol: a standard system that regulates the way in which information is transferred between computers

firewall: a security device that prevents unauthorized users from gaining access to a computer network

THE INTERNET AND INTRANETS

The Internet and intranets share some common features, yet they differ in some important respects. The Internet is a global, public **network** that connects hundreds of millions of computers. It is used to access information by everyone who has a computer connected to a network. Like the Internet, an intranet is a network of computers that allows its users to share **data,** news, and opinions quickly and easily. The Internet uses the same standards as an intranet does to enable communication, such as **HyperText** Transfer **Protocol** (HTTP) or Transmission Control Protocol/Internet Protocol (TCP/IP). There are differences between the Internet and intranets, however. The Internet is more open. It is public and belongs to no single entity. In contrast, an intranet is usually set up as a closed, private means of sharing information within an institution, such as a business or university. An institution creates an intranet mainly for security reasons and keeps its information behind a **firewall** to protect it from outsiders. Unlike an intranet, the Internet is unsecured and can be used to share or steal information freely as well as to harm computer systems. Thus, although the Internet and an intranet both allow connected computers to share information, they are different in some crucial ways.

POSTREADING DISCUSSION QUESTIONS

1. *What is the topic sentence of the paragraph? Write it here.*

   _____

   _____

   _____

2. *Identify the controlling idea in the topic sentence. Write it here.*

   _____

   _____

   _____

3. *Circle the two main ideas introduced in the topic sentence (the things being compared). Underline the information in the paragraph that tells how the Internet and an intranet are the same. Draw a box around the information that tells how the Internet and an intranet are different.*

   _____

   _____

   _____

4. *Underline the concluding sentence. Can you find some important ideas or terms that are the same in both the topic sentence and the concluding sentence? Write them here.*

   _____

   _____

   _____

5. *TOEFL Practice*

   Where would you insert this sentence in the paragraph? (Make a *5 in the paragraph between the two sentences.)

   The World Wide Web is all of the resources and users on the Internet that are using the Hypertext Transfer Protocol.

Shareware Versus Commercial Software

PREREADING DISCUSSION QUESTIONS

1. *Have you ever purchased software for a computer?*

2. *Have you ever downloaded software from the Internet?*

EXERCISE

2

READING AND ANSWERING QUESTIONS

Read the paragraph about two kinds of computer programs. Then answer the questions.

SOURCE
2

software: programs, routines, and symbolic languages that control the way a computer works

copyright: the legal right of an author, composer, playwright, publisher, or distributor to exclusive publication, production, sale, or distribution of a literary, musical, dramatic, or artistic work.

virus: a computer program that copies itself into the other programs stored in a computer; may be neutral or have a negative effect, such as causing a program to work incorrectly or corrupting a computer's memory.

bug: a defect in the code of a computer program

SHAREWARE VERSUS COMMERCIAL SOFTWARE

Commercial **software** and shareware are two kinds of computer programs that can be very similar in terms of their function yet are acquired and used differently. A commercial software program is **copyrighted** and available in retail stores for purchase. It offers instructions for use in the form of printed material that comes with the program as well as additional information in digital files within the program. Commercial software also comes with support, which means that the user can ask for assistance in learning how to use the program by contacting technical support by phone or e-mail. Like commercial software, shareware is copyrighted, but it is distributed freely on a trial basis, usually with the condition that the user pay a fee for continued use and support. In contrast with commercial software, shareware is typically smaller and simpler. It may or may not come with support and may even contain **viruses** or **bugs.** Rather than being purchased in a box at a store, shareware is downloaded from a web site for free. The user is able to try it for a while without cost until the trial period is over, usually 30 days. After the trial period, the user must pay a modest fee to continue to use it. Whereas shareware is more convenient and less expensive than commercial software, it may be less reliable and offer fewer options to users in its operation.

POSTREADING DISCUSSION QUESTIONS

1. What is the topic sentence of the paragraph? Write it here.

_____

_____

_____

2. Identify the controlling idea in the topic sentence. Write it here.

_____

_____

_____

3. Circle all of the words or phrases in the paragraph that indicate a shift in ideas. These are transition words and phrases that alert the reader to the similarities and differences between shareware and commercial software.

_____

_____

_____

4. TOEFL Practice

Where would you insert this sentence in the paragraph? (Make a *4 in the paragraph.)

A Uniform Resource Locator (URL) is the web address, or location of a web page in cyberspace, and usually includes the access protocol (http) and the domain name (such as www.hmco.com).

Organization in Comparison/Contrast Paragraphs

Comparison/contrast paragraphs can be organized in two ways:

▶ Alternate the discussion of the two ideas on a point-by-point basis.

▶ Divide the information into two parts, each part describing one of the two ideas or things being compared.

Study the following outlines to see how to organize a comparison/contrast paragraph first point by point and then in two parts.

TOPIC: The Digital Divide in the United States and in Third-World Countries

Point by Point

I. Lack of computers
    A. In economically deprived areas of the United States
    B. In third world countries

II. Lack of network infrastructure
  A. In economically deprived areas of the United States
  B. In third world countries

III. Lack of technical training
  A. In economically deprived areas of the United States
  B. In third world countries

Two-Part

I. The digital divide in economically deprived areas of the United States
  A. Lack of computers
  B. Lack of network infrastructure
  C. Lack of technical training

II. The digital divide in third world countries
  A. Lack of computers
  B. Lack of network infrastructure
  C. Lack of technical training

EXERCISE

3

REWRITING FOR ORGANIZATION

Reread Sources 1 and 2. Note that Source 1 on page 122 is organized by the point-by-point method, and Source 2 on page 124 is organized into two parts. On the lines below, rewrite the Source 1 paragraph using two-part organization. Use this outline to assist you. A few sentences have been added to get you started.

I. Similarities between the Internet and an intranet
  A. A network of computers
  B. Use standard Internet protocols, such as Hypertext Transfer Protocol (HTTP) or Transfer Connection Protocol/ Internet Protocol (TCP/IP)
  C. Share data, news, and opinions
  D. Share information efficiently and quickly

II. Differences between the Internet and an intranet
  A. Centralized vs. decentralized
  B. Public vs. private
  C. Unsecured vs. secure
  D. Open vs. closed

Intranets and the Internet share some common features, yet they differ in some important respects. Some of the similarities involve . . .

_____

_____

_____

_____

_____

_____

_____

_____

However, there are some major differences between the two systems.

_____

_____

_____

_____

_____

_____

_____

Transition Expressions

In a comparison/contrast paragraph, transition words can act as signals to the reader that a shift in thinking is about to take place.

Unit 5 Transition Expressions: *like, the same . . . as, in contrast,* and *whereas*

Expressions for Comparing

like

>   **Function:** shows that something possesses the same characteristics as, or is similar to

>   **Use:** *Like* can be used as a preposition to show that two things are similar.

(continued)

(continued)

Examples: <u>Like</u> her sister, Keira has blonde hair.

Bob has a silver car <u>like</u> his wife's car.

Practice: Find the sentence in Source 1 that contains the word *like*. Write it here.

_____

Find the sentence in Source 2 that contains the word *like*. Write it here.

_____

the same . . . as

Function: indicates someone or something similar in kind, quality, quantity, or degree

Use: *The same . . . as* is an adjective phrase that expresses how two things or ideas are alike.

Examples: We used <u>*the same*</u> book <u>*as*</u> we had in the previous class.

This song has <u>*the same*</u> tune <u>*as*</u> the song we heard earlier today.

Grammar Note: An adjective modifies a noun in a sentence. Therefore, when *the same . . . as* is used as an adjective phrase, a noun must come between *the same* and *as*.

Practice: Find the sentence in Source 1 that contains the phrase *the same . . . as*. Write it here.

_____

Expressions for Contrasting

in contrast

Function: shows differences when comparing

Use: *In contrast* is a prepositional phrase that shows that two things are different.

Examples: Educational institutions develop educational web sites. <u>*In contrast,*</u> commercial web sites are created by businesses.

Cats, <u>*in contrast*</u> with dogs, are more independent.

Grammar Note: When *in contrast* appears between two independent clauses in a compound sentence, a semicolon comes before *in contrast*, and a comma comes after it.

(continued)

(continued)

Example: My children love Middle Eastern food; *in contrast,* my parents do not like it.

When *in contrast* comes at the beginning of the sentence, a comma comes after it.

Example: This web site includes lots of graphic images. *In contrast,* that site includes only text.

If *in contrast* occurs in the middle of the sentence, put a comma on either side of it.

Example: The first candidate we interviewed for the new position looked promising; the second candidate, *in contrast,* did not seem as qualified.

Practice: Find the sentence in Source 1 that contains the phrase *in contrast.* Write it here.

_____

Find the sentence in Source 2 that contains the phrase *in contrast.* Write it here.

_____

whereas

Function: indicates the contrary to something just stated

Use: *Whereas* is a conjunction showing that two ideas or things are contrary.

Examples: <u>Whereas</u> Alasdair rarely takes a vacation, Lisa travels a lot.

I love to go to the movies <u>whereas</u> Valerie prefers to watch videos at home.

Grammar Note: Because *whereas* shows contrast, it needs a comma to separate the two contrasting parts of the sentence.

Example: I study with the radio on <u>whereas</u> my roommate likes it quiet.

Practice: Find the sentence in Source 1 that contains the word *whereas.* Write it here.

_____

Find the sentence in Source 2 that contains the word *whereas.* Write it here.

_____

(continued)

EXERCISE

WORKING WITH TRANSITION EXPRESSIONS

Read the paragraph. Fill in the blank with like, the same . . . as, in contrast, or whereas.

1. _____ the other students in the class, she was working on her web site.

2. In most parts of the United States, Internet access is available for free in public libraries. _____, the Internet is inaccessible in many parts of the developing world.

3. The colors on his web page are _____ the colors in his logo.

4. _____ Kim has been using the Internet at work for years, Ellen has never used the Internet for work purposes.

5. This news web site is showing _____ news story on the front page _____ the two web sites we checked.

6. _____ the other pages on this web site, this one has a green navigational tool bar.

7. _____ many electronic businesses online, ours has banner advertisements on many web pages.

8. _____ some people go out to nightclubs on the weekends, others meet new friends in chat rooms online.

9. In urban areas in the United States, many women now have cellular phones. _____, many women do not have cellular phones in rural areas.

10. Lisa bought _____ software _____ Paula did.

Paraphrasing, Summarizing, and Synthesizing

Before you continue, review these important skills in Unit 1, pages 14–25.

Paraphrasing: An Important Composition Skill

(For information about paraphrasing and a list of verbs to use when you introduce information from a source, see Unit 1, pages 14–15.)

EXERCISE
4

Paraphrasing Practice

*Read the original sentence. Then read the three possible paraphrases. Mark one **B** (BEST), one **TS** (TOO SIMILAR), and one **D** (DIFFERENT–or wrong–information).*

SOURCE **1** Page 122

1. Intranets and the Internet share some common features, yet they differ in some important aspects.

     _____ A. Though intranets and the Internet are similar, important differences exist between them.

     _____ B. The Internet is now a common feature of daily life, but intranets are different.

     _____ C. The Internet and intranets are similar, but they differ in several notable aspects.

2. An institution creates an intranet mainly for security reasons and keeps its information behind a firewall to protect it from outsiders.

     _____ A. For security reasons, an institution may create an intranet to keep its information behind a firewall to protect it from outsiders.

     _____ B. A firewall is a type of security scheme that prevents anyone who is not employed by a school or business from accessing information.

     _____ C. To keep its information safe and secure, a business or university creates an intranet, which uses a firewall to prevent unknown persons from getting information.

SOURCE **2** Page 124

3. Commercial software also comes with support, which means that the user can ask for assistance in learning how to use the program by contacting technical support by phone or e-mail.

     _____ A. Commercial software comes with support too, which means that one can ask for assistance through contacting technical support by phone or e-mail.

     _____ B. By making a phone call or sending an e-mail message, users of commercial software can request help in using the program from a technical specialists at a "help desk."

_____ C. Those who buy commercial software can often sit on the phone for half an hour or even longer waiting for someone to help with instructions for installing or using software.

4. It may or may not come with support and may even contain viruses or bugs.

_____ A. Viruses, otherwise known as "bugs," are the work of troublemakers and constitute a serious problem in the computing world.

_____ B. It may come with support or it may not and might even contain viruses or bugs.

_____ C. One must be cautious when considering downloading shareware because it may not come with complete instructions and might contain harmful computer viruses.

EXERCISE

5

PARAPHRASING PRACTICE

Read these original sentences from Sources 1 and 2. Circle what you consider to be the most important ideas. Then in number 1, choose the best paraphrase for the original sentence. In number 2, write your own paraphrase of the sentence. (See Unit 1, pages 14–15, for more information on paraphrasing.)

SOURCE 1
Page 122

1. Unlike an intranet, the Internet is unsecured and can be used to freely share or steal information as well as to harm computer systems.

_____ A. The Internet, in contrast to an intranet, is a place to share or take information that is not secure, and to send or receive viruses.

_____ B. Unlike an intranet, the Internet is not secured, and people can share or steal information freely and also do harm to computers and their systems.

_____ C. The Internet is an unvalidated source of free information and computer viruses, whereas an intranet is not.

SOURCE 2
Page 124

2. Like commercial software, shareware is copyrighted, but it is distributed freely on a trial basis, usually with the condition that the user pays a fee for continued use and support.

Your paraphrase:

_____

_____

_____

Summarizing

(For information about and guidelines for summarizing, see Unit 1, pages 18–21.)

EXERCISE

SUMMARIZING: FINDING THE MOST IMPORTANT IDEAS

Reread Source 1. Then make a list of up to six important facts or ideas in this paragraph. Use your paraphrasing skills, and do not copy word for word. It is not necessary to use complete sentences.

1. _____

_____

_____

2. _____

_____

_____

3. _____

_____

_____

4. _____

_____

_____

5. _____

_____

_____

6. _____

_____

_____

EXERCISE

7

SUMMARIZING: PUTTING IT IN YOUR OWN WORDS

Source 2 contains 233 words. Summarize the paragraph in approximately 50 words. Follow the steps presented in Unit 1, pages 18–21, to write your summary. Use correct paragraph format, including a topic sentence (see Unit 1, pages 18–21). You should write no more than five sentences in your summary. Remember that you must write the information in your own words.

_____

_____

_____

_____

_____

_____

_____

Synthesizing

To review the steps in synthesizing, see Unit 1, page 22, and Unit 2, page 53.

EXERCISE

8

PREPARING TO SYNTHESIZE

You will be synthesizing information from Sources 1 and 2 in Exercise 9. To prepare for that task, make notes below about one main idea from each source. Try to keep your notes about the main idea from each source to only three supporting ideas.

SOURCE

1

Page 122

The Internet

1. _____

_____

2. _____

_____

3. _____

_____

SOURCE
2
Page 124

Shareware

1. _____

_____

2. _____

_____

3. _____

_____

EXERCISE

9

SYNTHESIZING: EXAM QUESTION PRACTICE

Imagine that you are a student in a computer science class. In a comparison/contrast paragraph of four to eight sentences, write your answer to the following exam question. Synthesize the information from Sources 1 and 2 about the Internet and shareware. Use your notes from Exercise 8, and see Unit 1, page 22, for more information about synthesizing.

COMPUTER SCIENCE EXAM QUESTION:

How is the network of computers that we know as the Internet both different from and similar to shareware software? Write a paragraph comparing and contrasting these two ways of sharing information.

_____

_____

_____

_____

_____

_____

_____

_____

_____

_____

_____

_____

_____

_____

_____

_____

_____

_____

_____

_____

_____

The Writing Process: Practice Writing Comparison/Contrast Paragraphs

Objectives	**In Part B, you will:**
Prewriting:	answer open-ended questions to generate ideas
Planning:	list similarities and differences in a chart
First draft:	write a comparison/contrast paragraph
Peer reviewing:	review classmates' paragraphs and analyze feedback
Second draft:	use peer feedback to write a second draft
Editing:	
Grammar Focus:	practice using *comparatives* and *superlatives*
Sentence Check:	identify and practice writing using dependent noun clauses
Mechanics:	capitalization of titles
Final draft:	complete the final draft of a comparison/contrast paragraph

The Writing Process: Writing Assignment

Your assignment is to write a comparison/contrast paragraph of five to ten sentences about the roles of men and the roles of women in the home in your native country.

Prewriting: Answering Open-Ended Questions to Generate Ideas

Answering open-ended questions can help you focus your ideas for writing. In the next exercise, you will jot down responses to questions with a partner and compare your responses to get ideas for writing your comparison/contrast paragraph. After you have answered these questions and reviewed them with a partner, you will identify the ideas that you want to use in your paragraph.

EXERCISE 10

USING PREWRITING STRATEGIES

Get Started:
Answer the open-ended questions below. Don't be concerned about using complete sentences at this point.

1. What are the common household chores of a family in your country?

   _____

   _____

   _____

2. Which of these tasks involve physical labor?

   _____

   _____

   _____

3. Which tasks involve intellectual know-how?

   _____

   _____

4. Which gender usually performs the tasks you listed in Question 2?

   _____

   In Question 3?_____

   _____

5. Why do you think this is so? (Your answer to this question may form your conclusion to your paragraph.)

   _____

   _____

   _____

   _____

Identify Related Ideas:

Now get together with a partner and share your responses to the five questions in Exercise 10. Use the following questions to guide your discussion.

▶ Did you have any of the same ideas as your partner?

▶ Which ideas were different?

▶ Do you agree with your partner's ideas that were different from yours?

▶ Which ideas do you want to keep for your paragraph?

▶ Which ideas might you like to include from your partner's responses?

Add any new ideas to your responses, and circle all ideas that you want to use in your paragraph.

Planning: Listing Similarities and Differences in a Chart

Use the following chart to list the similarities and differences between the roles and responsibilities of women and men inside the home. This chart outlines a comparison/contrast paragraph in the two-part method. (see page 126).

Similarities Between Men's and Women's Responsibilities Inside the Home

I. _____

II. _____

III. _____

Differences Between Men's and Women's Responsibilities Inside the Home

I. _____

II. _____

III. _____

First Draft

You are now ready to write the first draft of your paragraph. As a guideline, use the ideas from the chart you just completed and write complete sentences in paragraph form. Remember to use the transition expressions *like, the same . . . as, in contrast,* and *whereas.*

Keep these things in mind as you write:

▶ Begin with a topic sentence that includes a controlling idea. Your topic sentence should include the main idea you want the reader to understand about the domestic roles and responsibilities of men and women in your native country.

▶ Remember that comparison/contrast paragraphs include both similarities and differences.

▶ Because you are organizing your ideas using the two-part method, use transition words and phrases in moving from one idea to the next to show how the ideas are similar or different.

First Draft Checklist

When you finish your paragraph, use this checklist to review your writing.

First Draft Checklist

1. Do I have a topic sentence that contains a clear topic and controlling idea?

2. Are all the sentences about the topic?

3. How are my main ideas (women's work and men's work inside the home) both similar and different from each other?

4. Have I used transition words correctly to show differences and similarities in my ideas?

5. Does my concluding sentence sum up the paragraph or express feelings?

6. Did I format my paragraph correctly?

Peer Review

Exchange papers with another student. Read your partner's paper and answer the questions on Partner Feedback Form: Unit 5, pages 201–202. Discuss your partner's reactions to your paragraph. Make notes about any parts you need to change in your second draft.

Second Draft

Remember that second draft revising should include more than grammar, punctuation, and spelling corrections. You should also be checking the topic sentence, the supporting details, the concluding sentence, and the overall completeness and clarity of your paragraph. Now carefully revise your paragraph, using feedback from your partner and your own ideas for revising.

Second Draft Checklist I

1. Is my topic sentence easy for the reader to understand?

2. Does the topic sentence include the two main ideas that are being compared?

3. Are all the sentences about this topic? Is there any sentence that does not belong here?

4. Are all the sentences about similarities together and all of the sentences about differences together?

5. How many transition expressions are there? (Underline them.)

6. Are there transitions that show a shift in ideas from similarities to differences? Add them if needed.

7. Have I considered all my partner's comments and suggestions?

Editing: Grammar and Mechanics

Reviewing and practicing the following grammatical points will help you self-edit your paragraph for common grammatical mistakes.

Grammar Focus: Comparatives and Superlatives

Comparatives

In English, adjectives are used to compare two ideas, things, or people. Below are some comparative forms:

adjective + *-er* + *than*	OR	*more/less* + adjective + *than*
slower than		more fascinating than
saltier than		less complicated than

Comparative adjectives compare two people, places, things, or ideas.

> *Example:*
>
> The soup was <u>saltier than</u> the vegetables.
>
> The novel was <u>more fascinating than</u> the film version of the story.

EXERCISE

11

USING COMPARATIVE ADJECTIVES

Complete the sentences with the correct form of the adjective. Use more or -er than when you see a plus sign (+). Use less than when you see a minus sign (−). Follow the patterns in the blue shaded area above with the exception of one form, which is irregular. The first one has been done for you.

1. Compared with the situation even twenty years ago, women are in governmental positions that are _more important than_ (+ important) they were before.

2. When making a point in a meeting, women are often _____ (– forceful) men.

3. Possibilities for women to advance in their careers are certainly _____ (+ good) they were in the past.

4. Home life for men today in the United States is _____ (+ hard) in the 1950s. Nowadays, men often must do housework, cook, and care for children, just as women do.

5. Women who work part-time are often _____ (+ happy) full-time workers with respect to their work and family responsibilities.

6. Pressures on women to balance family and work are often _____ (+ strong) those on men.

7. Some people believe that women are _____ (+ patient) men when caring for children.

8. Stepfathers in the United States are usually _____ (+ close) stepmothers to their stepchildren emotionally.

9. This is because stepmothers are _____ (– able) stepfathers to spend time with their stepchildren because stepfathers live with their stepchildren more often than stepmothers do.

10. Family life in the United States is certainly _____ (+ complicated) it used to be in the past.

Superlatives

In English, adjectives are used to compare two ideas, things, or people. These are the superlative forms:

the + adjective + *-est*	OR	*the* + most/least + adjective/
the slowest		the most fascinating
the saltiest		the least complicated

Superlative adjectives show which is first or last in a group of three or more. They show the ultimate differences in the group.

Examples:

The soup was <u>the saltiest</u> of all the dishes.

That novel was <u>the least fascinating</u> of those I read last summer.

EXERCISE

12

USING SUPERLATIVE ADJECTIVES

Write sentences with a superlative adjective, giving your opinion about each of the following ideas. The first one has been done for you.

1. Urgent world problem

   The most urgent world problem is the spread

   of HIV/AIDS.

2. Good way to care for children

   _____

   _____

3. Boring academic field of study

   _____

   _____

4. Beautiful city in the world

   _____

   _____

5. Expensive present you received

   _____

   _____

6. Bad movie you have seen

   _____

   _____

7. Easy meal to prepare

   _____

   _____

8. Enjoyable evening

_____

_____

9. Distasteful chore in the house

_____

_____

10. Long novel you read

_____

_____

As . . . as and _the same . . . as_ **with Adjectives, Adverbs and Nouns**

To compare and contrast, we use _as . . . as_ in the following ways.

1. Use _as_ + adjective + _as_ to show that two people, places, or ideas are equal or similar.

    Example: Tonight the stars are <u>as bright as</u> they were last night.

2. Use _as_ + adverb + _as_ to show that two actions or situations are equal or similar.

    Example: He hit the tennis ball <u>as forcefully as</u> his partner did.

3. Use the negative form of the verb + _as . . . as_ to show differences.

    Example: John <u>is not as old as</u> Bill.

4. Use _the same_ + noun + _as_ to show equality.

    Example: I have <u>the same umbrella as</u> you do.

EXERCISE

13

WRITING SENTENCES WITH AS . . . AS

Crocodiles and alligators are similar in some ways and different in others. Write five sentences about crocodiles and alligators. Use the information in the charts and follow the examples below.

crocodile

alligator

	Crocodiles and Alligators
SAME	▶ Both are dangerous reptiles ▶ Both belong to the family Crocodilidae ▶ Both live in warm, swampy areas in the United States ▶ Both have jaws that are hinged on the bottom

	Crocodiles	Alligators
DIFFERENT	▶ Live in salt water and have salt-extracting glands ▶ Fourth tooth on lower jaw sticks out ▶ Very aggressive ▶ Can live to be 100 years old	▶ Are unable to live in salt water for long periods ▶ All teeth are hidden when mouth is closed ▶ Not as aggressive ▶ Can live to be 50 years old

Example sentences:

The alligator does not live as long as the crocodile.

The jaws of an alligator work in the same way as the jaws of a crocodile.

1. _____

2. _____

3. _____

4. _____

5. _____

Sentence Check: Noun Clauses

Noun clauses function as nouns in sentences. Like all clauses, a noun clause includes a noun and a verb. Noun clauses can begin with *that* or a *wh-*word (*who, where, when, what,* or *why*). These words link the noun clause to the main clause of the sentence.

Examples:

I know that she is behind that door.

The note didn't say when they plan to leave tomorrow.

What people need to understand is that mad cow disease is a direct result of feeding animals materials from other diseased animals.

EXERCISE

14

IDENTIFYING NOUN CLAUSES

Read each sentence. Underline the noun clause, and circle the word that introduces it.

1. Bert's mother was concerned that he wasn't eating properly.
2. We don't know when the park will close.
3. Can you tell why the traffic light is yellow?
4. I want to know what the answer is.
5. Noah realized that the rest of the family had left him behind.
6. Anjali believes that she should wait a while to have children.
7. They cannot understand why the library closes so early.
8. I wonder who will repair the leak.
9. Did you notice where the snow is piling up?
10. Let's go see who is starring in the movie tonight.

EXERCISE

15

COMPLETING NOUN CLAUSES

Read the sentences and add a wh- word (who, where, when, what, or why) or that to each noun phrase. The first one has been done for you.

1. It is an understatement to say _____that_____ mad cow disease

   changed the way animals were treated and fed in the year 2001.

2. In addition, the fear of not knowing _____ animals

   were infected with this disease prompted new policies and

   procedures in moving animals from one country to another.

3. Not only were animals treated differently as a result of the outbreak

   of this disease, but because the government wanted to know

   _____ people were working, they were asked at airports

   whether they worked on farms or had traveled to farms recently.

4. The biggest change was _____ farmers were no longer feeding their animals food that was made from other animals' bones.

5. Farmers became more careful than they had been about _____ prepared the food for their animals.

Mechanics: Capitalization of Title Review

In Unit 3, you practiced the rules for writing titles. Here is a review of the capitalization rules.

You should capitalize:

▶ The first word

▶ The last word

▶ The first word after a colon indicating a subtitle

▶ The word after a hyphen in a compound word.

Otherwise, do **not** capitalize:

▶ Articles (*a, an, the*)

▶ Prepositions (*of, between, under, through,* etc.)

▶ Conjunctions (*and, but, for,* etc.)

▶ The *to* in an infinitive

Examples:

As You Like It

Writing Paragraphs: A Short Guide

Notes on the Observation of Drosophilae

The Tri-Petaled Flower

EXERCISE

16

TITLE CAPITALIZATION REVIEW

Correct these titles by making changes in capitalization as necessary.

1. Go Tell it on the Mountain

2. Get A Life

3. Your Guide to the museums of Europe

4. A New Look at Renewable Energy Sources: a Response to the Bush Energy Plan

5. The Provinces Of The Roman Empire

Return to Your Second Draft

Now look at your second draft again and check these items. Make corrections where necessary.

Second Draft Checklist II

1. Are all of your noun clauses formed correctly?

2. Have you used comparative and superlative adjectives correctly in your paragraph?

3. Have you used commas correctly with your transition words and phrases?

4. Check carefully for run-on sentences, comma splices, and fragments. (See Appendix 2, Appendix 3, and Appendix 4 for more information on these three sentence problems.)

5. Did you include a title for your paragraph? If not, add one now, paying careful attention to capitalization rules.

6. Work with a partner on the Partner Feedback Form again. Make corrections where necessary.

Final Draft

Carefully revise your paragraph, using all of the feedback you have received: partner feedback review, instructor comments, and self-evaluation. In addition, try reading your paragraph aloud. This can help you find awkward-sounding sentences and errors in punctuation. When you have finished, neatly type your final draft.

Additional Writing Assignments from the Academic Disciplines

Beginning with the prewriting activity on page 139, go through the steps of writing another comparison/contrast paragraph. Choose a topic from the following list.

SUBJECT	*WRITING TASK*
Business	Compare and contrast the management styles of managers in the United States and in another country.
Culture	Compare and contrast the ways in which the celebration of two holidays is commercialized.
Media studies	Compare and contrast the broadcast of the same international news story as it is reported by an Internet source from the United States and one from another country.
Health care	Compare and contrast giving birth in a hospital to giving birth at home with a midwife.

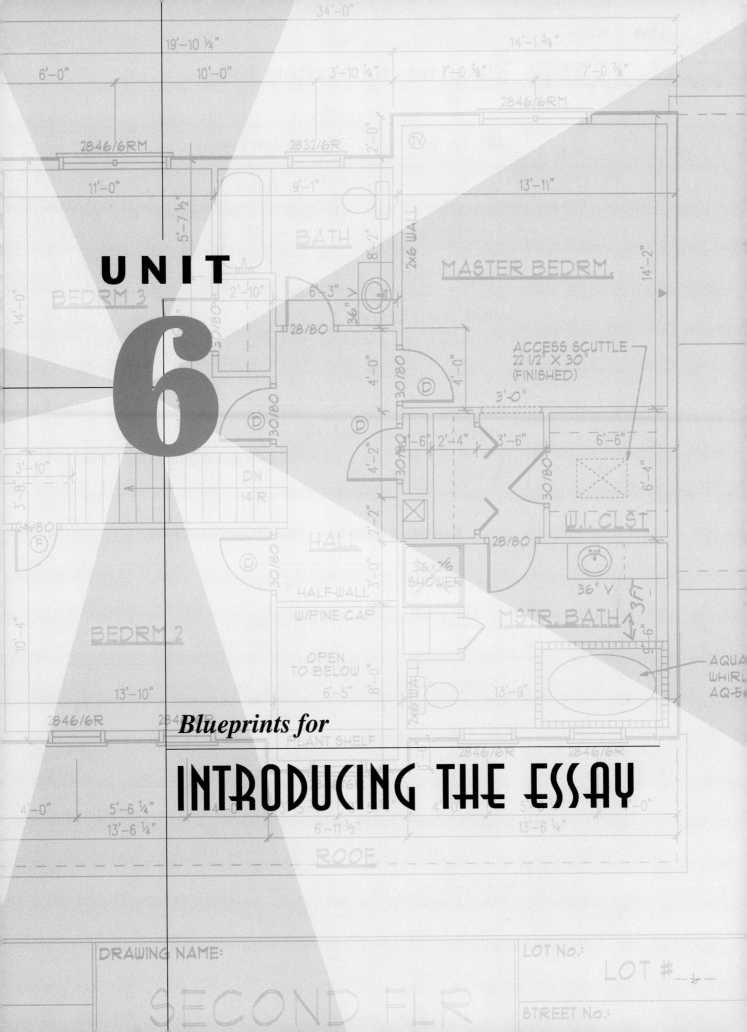

UNIT 6

Blueprints for

INTRODUCING THE ESSAY

PART A Blueprints for Writing Essays

Objectives	In Part A, you will:
Analysis:	note the differences between a paragraph and an essay
Transitions:	learn transition expressions for essay writing
Practice:	work with essay outlines

What Is an Essay?

An essay is a group of paragraphs—usually about four to seven—that is about one topic. Whereas a paragraph deals with a small area of a topic, an essay can include several aspects of a topic. The organization of an essay is similar to that of a single paragraph.

Comparing Paragraphs and Essays

Study the following chart that comparisons paragraphs and essays. Then read the explanation below it.

Overview Comparison of Paragraphs and Essays

Paragraph	Essay
Topic sentence	Introductory paragraph + THESIS STATEMENT
Supporting sentences/details	Supporting paragraphs with topic sentences + supporting sentences/details
Concluding sentence	Concluding paragraph

What tells the reader the content and organization of the writing?	*Paragraph:* A paragraph contains a *topic sentence*, which is the guiding sentence for the paragraph. *Essay:* An essay contains a similar sentence, but it is called the *thesis statement*. The function of the thesis statement is the same as that of the topic sentence, but it is not the first sentence in the essay.
What makes up the body of the writing?	*Paragraph:* A paragraph contains supporting *sentences.* *Essay:* An essay contains supporting *paragraphs.*
What ends the writing?	*Paragraph:* A paragraph has a concluding *sentence.* *Essay:* An essay has a concluding *paragraph.*

Comparison of Essay and Paragraph Organization

Essay Organization	Paragraph Organization
Introductory paragraph (contains the *hook*) Thesis statement: usually between two and five ideas (points of development) =	Topic sentence
Supporting paragraph 1 (idea 1) = Topic sentence + supporting details	Supporting details
Transition sentence Supporting paragraph 2 (idea 2) = Topic sentence + supporting details	Supporting details (continued)

(continued) Transition sentence Supporting paragraph 3 (idea 3) Topic sentence + supporting details	=	Supporting details
Transition sentence Concluding paragraph	=	Concluding sentence

Introductory Paragraph

Like a paragraph, an essay has one topic, which is presented in the **introductory paragraph.** Writers often begin this first paragraph with a **hook,** which can be an interesting quote, a statistic, or a catchy phrase to get the reader interested. It leads the reader to the **thesis statement,** the main idea about the topic. The thesis statement generally contains two to five ideas or points of development about the topic that the writer will discuss in the essay. Each of these ideas usually has a corresponding supporting paragraph in the essay.

Supporting Paragraph 1

The second paragraph is **supporting paragraph** 1. It is about the **first idea** in the thesis statement. This paragraph, like all paragraphs, has its own **topic sentence and supporting details.** The whole paragraph supports the main topic of the essay. Good writers include a **transition sentence** (the concluding sentence of the paragraph) that sums up the information in this paragraph and leads into the next paragraph.

Supporting Paragraphs 2 to 5

In the rest of the supporting paragraphs, the writer discusses **ideas 2 to 5** of the thesis statement (which is found in the introductory paragraph). Each paragraph has its own topic sentence and supporting details. Each paragraph supports the main topic of the essay. The transition sentence (the concluding sentence of the paragraph) sums up the information in this paragraph and leads into the final paragraph of the essay.

Concluding Paragraph

The **concluding paragraph** of an essay is similar to the concluding sentence of a paragraph, but it relates to all the ideas in the thesis statement. The concluding paragraph might restate the thesis statement. It might also give an opinion or suggestion about the thesis statement. This paragraph usually goes from specific information to general information.

EXERCISE	
1	

PARAGRAPHS AND ESSAYS QUIZ

Answer the following questions based on the information you just studied about essays and paragraphs.

1. What is the first paragraph in an essay called?

   _____

2. What are some good examples of "hooks" to introduce an essay?

   _____

   _____

   _____

3. What sentence in an essay is like the topic sentence in a paragraph?

   _____

4. In an essay, what is the first sentence of each supporting paragraph
   called? (Note: Sometimes it is not the first sentence.)

   _____

5. What are the possible functions of the final paragraph in an essay?

   a. _____

   b. _____

   c. _____

From Paragraph to Essay: An Example

The following paragraph is from Unit 1, pages 4–5. Reread it here. Then read "Global Marketing Strategies," which expands the topic of the paragraph into an essay.

PARAGRAPH FROM UNIT 1

Selling a product successfully in another country often requires changes in the original product. Domino's Pizza offers mayonnaise and potato pizza in Tokyo and pickled ginger pizza in India. Heinz varies its ketchup recipe to satisfy the needs of specific markets. In Belgium and Holland, for example, the ketchup is not as sweet as it is in the United States. When Haagen-Dazs served up one of its most popular American flavors, Chocolate Chip Cookie Dough, to British customers, they left it sitting in supermarket freezers. What the premium ice cream maker learned is that chocolate chip cookies aren't popular in Great Britain, and children don't have a history of snatching raw dough from the bowl, so the company had to develop flavors that would sell in Great Britain. After holding a contest to come up with a flavor the British would like, the company launched "Cool

Britannia," vanilla ice cream with strawberries and chocolate-covered Scottish shortbread. Because dairy products are not part of Chinese diets, Frito-Lay took the cheese out of Chee-tos in China. Instead, the company sells Seafood Chee-tos. Without a doubt, these products were so successful in these foreign lands only because the company realized that it was wise to do market research and make fundamental changes in the products.

GLOBAL MARKETING STRATEGIES

1   A commonly heard phrase these days is "global village." This expression generally refers to information that is available everywhere in the world. In business and marketing, this phrase can refer to global marketing and the selling of a product or service. Companies large and small have been trying to break into new markets for many years, but some companies have been more successful than others. Some companies have a broader knowledge of how to make their products sell to international customers. Selling a product successfully in another country often requires making changes in the product such as adding ingredients, replacing existing ingredients, and making completely new versions.

← IDEA 1

IDEA 3 →

IDEA 2 →

2   One way in which companies attempt to sell their products is by adding ingredients to their original products to make them more **appealing to** the local consumers. For example, in Japan, Domino's Pizza sells pizzas with **toppings** such as mayonnaise, potatoes, and tuna. Because these items are so popular with the Japanese, Domino's can be almost certain that these specialty pizzas will be more successful than their American **counterparts.** Domino's has had similar success marketing their pizzas in India. Indian cuisine is known worldwide for being spicy, and Domino's used that knowledge to appeal to the **target market** by creating pickled ginger pizzas. This method is often successful in **enticing** locals into trying new products that contain a familiar flavor.

3   Another method of increasing sales abroad is replacing original ingredients with others that are more appealing to the local consumers. For instance, the Frito-Lay company, when attempting to introduce its

appealing to: likeable, agreeable

toppings: additional items put on top of certain types of foods

counterparts: something that is corresponding or complementary

target market: a group of consumers chosen to buy a certain product

enticing: alluring, tempting

(continued)

(continued)

Chee-tos brand snack foods in China, had to change its main ingredient, cheese. The Chinese are not big consumers of cheese. As a result, the cheese was taken out of Chee-tos and replaced with seafood. The new product, Seafood Chee-tos, is now one of the largest-selling snack foods in China.

4 <u>Finally, some companies choose to make a completely new version for the market.</u> One of the most popular ice cream flavors to come out on the United States market for Haagen-Dazs is Chocolate Chip Cookie Dough. Most people in the United States can remember tasting their mother's chocolate chip cookie dough before it was put in the oven. However, when Haagen-Dazs tried marketing this flavor in Great Britain, the product sat on the shelves. This happened because, in Britain, people were unfamiliar with the concept of eating raw cookie dough. As a result, Haagen-Dazs held a contest to come up with a brand-new "British" variety of ice cream. The winner was **eventually** labeled "Cool Britannia" and **featured** vanilla ice cream, strawberries, and chocolate-covered Scottish shortbread. Would this flavor be as successful in the United States? The answer is probably no because Americans are not **accustomed to** eating the slightly salty shortbread that is so popular in Great Britain.

5 It is **evident** that to be successful around the globe, companies must adapt their products to suit the needs of their **universal** customers. Some common ways are to add local ingredients, replace original ingredients, or make brand-new versions of the original product. Without a doubt, products such as Domino's pizza and Chee-tos were able to succeed in these foreign lands because the companies realized the importance of market research. Because these **fundamental** market **characteristics** were taken into account, these products **flourished** overseas.

eventually: ultimately, finally, some time afterward

featured: highlighted, promoted

accustomed to: used to, familiar with

evident: apparent, clear

universal: global

fundamental: essential, basic

characteristics: traits, qualities

flourished: prospered, succeeded

EXERCISE

2

UNDERSTANDING ESSAY ORGANIZATION

Write an answer for each item below.

THE THESIS STATEMENT

1. Reread the first paragraph of "Global Marketing Strategies." The underlined sentence is called the thesis statement. Write it here.

_____

_____

_____

2. What does the thesis statement tell the reader?

_____

_____

_____

3. What is the hook in this essay? Write it here.

_____

_____

_____

TOPIC SENTENCES WITHIN THE ESSAY

4. Reread paragraph 2 and note the underlined topic sentence. What does this paragraph discuss?

_____

_____

_____

5. Reread paragraph 3 and note the underlined topic sentence. What does this paragraph discuss?

_____

_____

_____

6. Reread paragraph 4 and note the underlined topic sentence. What does this paragraph discuss?

_____

_____

_____

SUPPORTING DETAILS

7. How do the topic sentences in paragraphs 1, 2, and 3 support the thesis statement?

_____

_____

_____

CONCLUDING PARAGRAPH

8. Read the first two sentences of paragraph 5. Which sentence restates the thesis statement (from paragraph 1)? Write it here.

   _____

   _____

9. The final sentences in the essay give an opinion about the topic of global marketing. What does the author say about the importance of changing a product to sell it in a foreign market?

   _____

   _____

EXERCISE

3

COMPARING A PARAGRAPH AND AN ESSAY

The information in the following list from the paragraph about global marketing (pages 153–154) has also been incorporated into the essay (page 154) on global marketing. Write the information in the proper category. The first one has been done for you. (You may refer to the essay to help you locate the information.)

Chocolate Chip Cookie dough ice cream   potato pizza

Seafood Chee-tos   ginger pizza

Cool Britannia ice cream

   1. Adding ingredients: *potato pizza,* _____

   2. Replacing ingredients: _____

   3. Inventing products: _____

Transition Expressions

   In the same way that transition expressions indicate a shift from one idea to another in a paragraph, transition expressions in essays show a shift in ideas within an essay, making your essay flow smoothly from one paragraph to another. Writers use transition expressions to connect paragraphs and ideas in essays the same way they use them to connect sentences and ideas in paragraphs. The correct use of transitions will add coherence (unity) to your writing.

(continued)

(continued)

Unit 6 Transition Expressions: *for example/for instance, one . . ., another . . ., such as*

for example/for instance

Function: gives an example of the previous point

Uses: *For example* and *for instance* mean the same thing and are interchangeable.

They are usually followed by a subject and a verb.

Punctuation note: At the beginning of a sentence, *for example* and *for instance* are followed by a comma.

Examples: There are many ways to become healthy. <u>For example</u>, a person can begin an exercise program.

Physics is a valuable tool for many occupations. <u>For instance</u>, engineers use the principles of physics on a regular basis.

For example and *for instance* can also come in the middle or at the end of the sentence.

Punctuation Note: In the middle of a sentence, the entire phrase is set off by commas.

Examples: There are many ways to become healthy. A person can, <u>for example</u>, begin an exercise program.

Physics is a valuable tool for many occupations. Engineers, <u>for instance</u>, use the principles of physics on a regular basis.

Punctuation Note: At the end of a sentence, the phrase is set off by a comma.

Examples: There are many ways to become healthy. A person can begin an exercise program, <u>for example</u>.

Physics is a valuable tool for many occupations. Engineers use the principles of physics on a regular basis, <u>for instance</u>.

Practice: In "Global Marketing Strategies," find the sentence in paragraph 2 that contains the phrase *for example*. Write it here.

_____

Find the sentence in paragraph 3 that contains the phrase *for instance*. Write it here.

_____

(continued)

(continued)

one (way/type/method/reason)

Function: gives the first specific example of the main point

Uses: *One . . .* can be followed by a number of expressions. The easiest is to add the verb *be + an infinitive.*

Example: There are many methods for losing weight. <u>One way is to eat</u> more vegetables.

Another form is to use an *infinitive + be + infinitive.*

Example: There are many methods for losing weight. <u>One way to lose weight is to eat</u> more vegetables.

Finally, you can use *that* or *which* to begin a clause.

Example: <u>One way that people can lose weight</u> is by eating more vegetables.

Practice: In "Global Marketing Strategies," find the sentence in Paragraph 2 that contains the phrase *one. . . .* Write it here.

---

another (method/way/type) of

Function: gives a subsequent specific example of the main point

Uses: *Another . . . of* is a noun phrase that can be in the subject slot of a sentence.

subject   gerund

Example: <u>Another method of losing weight</u> is to eat more vegetables.

subject   noun

<u>Another method of weight loss</u> is to eat more vegetables.

The *Another . . . of* phrase can also appear as the object in the sentence.

Example: Some dieters have tried "liquid diets," but these plans do not work well.

object   noun

These people need <u>another method of weight loss.</u>

Practice: In "Global Marketing Strategies," find the sentence in paragraph 3 that contains the phrase *another . . . of.* Write it here.

(continued)

(continued)

such as

Function: introduces examples of a previous point

Use: *Such as* can be followed by a single example or by a list of examples. If you give more than one example, the items in the list must be parallel, having the same grammatical structure (all nouns, all verbs, etc.).

Examples: Italian pasta such as tortellini can be a delicious alternative to plain spaghetti.

Professionals such as doctors, lawyers, and teachers often attend this charity event.

Grammar Note: Never begin a sentence with *such as*.

Practice: In "Global Marketing Strategies," find the sentence in paragraph 5 that contains the phrase *such as*. Write it here.

EXERCISE

WORKING WITH TRANSITION EXPRESSIONS

After you discuss the following questions with a partner, read the essay about the field of nursing. Then go back and fill in the blanks with transition expressions from the list in the box. Some transition expressions may fit into more than one blank.

PREREADING DISCUSSION QUESTIONS

1. *What do you know about the field of nursing?*

2. *Do you know anyone who works as a nurse?*

3. *What is your opinion about the nursing profession?*

one	for example	another
such as	for instance	

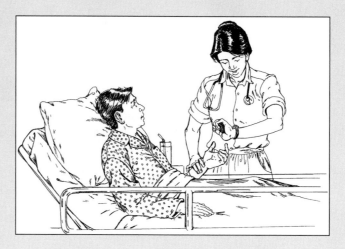

(continued)

(continued)

NURSING CHOICES

focus: center of interest or attention

1.   When deciding on a career, young people today tend to **focus** their energy on high-technology jobs. However, the field of nursing is growing and offers good pay, benefits, and job security. Qualified nurses are needed to fill many positions in hospitals, doctors' offices, private clinics, and specialty facilities. This profession is appropriate for many types of people, as there are many different types of nurses. The three most common classifications of nurses in the United States are Licensed Practical Nurse (LPN), Registered Nurse (RN), and Accredited Registered Nurse Practitioner (ARNP).

certification: the act of validating something with an official document

2.   Becoming a Licensed Practical Nurse requires the least amount of training. These nurses can receive **certification** after ten months of study in a vocational school. They can easily find employment in institutions **(1)** _____ hospitals, clinics, and doctors' offices. However, their responsibilities are rather limited. **(2)** _____, they are allowed to draw a patient's blood, take blood pressure, and insert **intravenous tubes** (IVs) or **catheters,** but they cannot supply narcotics or inject medication. Those duties fall to more qualified nurses.

intravenous tubes: tubes that carry fluids into a vein

catheters: tubes inserted into a duct in the body to carry fluids out

administering: giving

3. **(3)** _____ type of nursing program is the Registered Nurse program. RNs must complete at least a two-year nursing program (Associate of Science Degree). Some choose to continue for two more years and receive a Bachelor's Degree in Science. After getting their degrees, RNs can practice nursing. Their duties include **administering** medication (as well as narcotics) to patients and caring for them as assistants to the doctors.

(continued)

(continued)

RNs can be found in hospital wards, private clinics, and other areas. **(4)** _____ benefit of becoming an RN over an LPN is the salary. Registered Nurses have more responsibility than Licensed Practical Nurses, but their salary is higher as well.

4. Accredited Registered Nurse Practitioners are one step below doctors. ARNPs must earn not only a two-year degree (Associate of Science) but also a Bachelor's degree and a Master's. After six years of **intensive** study, nurse practitioners are able to complete many of the same tasks as doctors. **(5)** _____, they can set up office space in a doctor's office, have their own patients, and treat them in much the same way that a doctor can. Unfortunately, the salary difference between nurse practitioners and medical doctors is **vast,** with nurse practitioners receiving only a fraction of what doctors make.

5. The field of nursing is **diverse,** depending on individual preferences. Those who want a steady job but aren't interested in a long period of study can choose to enter the field as an LPN. People who want more responsibility in the field of medicine can study more intensively and become RNs or ARNPs. Because the need for medical care will always **remain,** this type of training will continue to be in demand.

intensive: deep or strong

vast: great in size

diverse: different

remain: continue the same

Working with Essay Outlines

Because writing an essay is a much longer process than writing a paragraph, good writers often work with outlines. Outlines help writers organize information and decide what order to put it in. Outlines also help writers keep their essays unified. Outlines group similar ideas into paragraphs and maintain coherence or unity in the information. When you work with an outline, do not worry about correct grammar or punctuation. That will come later in the essay-writing process. Study the following two examples of essay outlines.

examples

OUTLINE 1: TOPIC: POPULAR MOVIE GENRES

I. Introductory paragraph
    A. Hook
    B. Narrowing information toward the thesis (Because the hook is not always directly related to the topic, a few sentences are sometimes needed to make the connection between the hook and the thesis statement.)
    C. THESIS STATEMENT: Although the film industry continues to develop more and more film genres, the three most common

    1   **2**   **3**
    genres are drama , comedy, and science fiction .

                                                            1
II. Supporting paragraph 1: Topic sentence: dramatic movies are one popular form of film.
    A. Definition of drama
    B. Elements of drama
    C. Examples of successful dramatic films

                                                        2
III. Supporting paragraph 2. Topic sentence: Comedy is another genre of popular film.
    A. Definition of comedy
    B. Elements of comedy
    C. Examples of successful comedies

IV. Supporting paragraph 3. Topic sentence: In addition to dramas and
                              3
    comedies, science fiction films are extremely popular with the general public.
    A. Definition of science fiction
    B. Elements of science fiction
    C. Examples of successful science fiction films

V. Concluding paragraph (restates the thesis statement or gives an opinion or suggestion about the thesis statement)

OUTLINE 2: TOPIC: TYPES OF FATIGUE

I. Introductory paragraph
   A. Hook
   B. Narrowing information toward the thesis
   C. THESIS STATEMENT: The three most common types of fatigue
   are **physical** [1], **pathological** [2], and **psychological** [3].

II. Supporting paragraph 1: Topic sentence: One of the most common
   types of fatigue is **physical** [1].

   A. Description/symptoms: (after physical exertion) a person feels
      tired physically
      1. The person feels weak.
      2. Although tired, the person feels good.
   B. Cures:
      1. Rest
      2. Good eating habits
      3. Maintained exercise program

III. Supporting paragraph 2: Topic sentence: Another type of fatigue can
   be classified as **pathological** [2].

   A. Description/symptoms:
      1. A person feels tired mentally and physically.
      2. The fatigue does not go away after rest.
   B. Treatment:
      1. Medical evaluation
      2. Different types of therapy

IV. Supporting paragraph 3: Topic sentence: Finally, fatigue can be
   wholly **psychological** [3].

   A. Description/symptoms
      1. Weakness not connected to physical activity
      2. Weakness manifested emotionally
   B. Treatment:
      1. Medical evaluation
      2. Talk therapy
      3. Drug therapy

V. Concluding paragraph (restates the thesis statement or gives an
   opinion or suggestion about the thesis statement)

EXERCISE

WORKING WITH ESSAY OUTLINES

*Work with a partner. Read each essay topic and outline. Then fill in the
blanks with appropriate topic sentences and details. You might need to look
up some information in the library or on the Internet.*

TOPIC 1: THREE TYPES OF GOVERNING METHODS
FOR NATIONS

I.   Introductory paragraph

    A. Hook

    C. Narrowing information toward the thesis

    C. THESIS STATEMENT: Among all the countries of the world,

        the most common styles of leadership are **dictatorships** [1],

        monarchies [2], and **republics** [3].

II. Supporting paragraph 2: Topic sentence:

    _____

    _____

    _____

    A. How the government is structured

    B. Who has the most power

    C. Examples of countries with this style of leadership

III. Supporting paragraph 3: Topic sentence: Another style of leadership

    that is still found today is a **monarchy** [2].

    A. _____

       _____

    B. Who has the power

    C. _____

       _____

IV. Supporting paragraph 4: Topic sentence:

    _____

    _____

    _____

    A. Fundamentals of republic style governments

    B. The parts of this government

    C. _____

       _____

    D. Examples of countries with this style

V.   Concluding paragraph (restates the thesis statement or gives an
    opinion or suggestion about the thesis statement)

TOPIC 2: THREE BENEFITS OF HOME SCHOOLING:

I. Introductory paragraph
   A. Hook
   B. Narrowing information toward the thesis
   C. THESIS STATEMENT: Many parents realize the benefits of teaching their children at home rather than sending them to school, in particular the **curriculum options** [1], **the pacing** [2] **of the class** [2], and the **extra bonding between parents and** [3] **their children** [3].

II. Supporting paragraph 1: Topic sentence: Parents who teach their children at home have more freedom in choosing the subject matter or **curriculum** [1] for their children.

   A. They can focus on the interests of their children.
   B. They can add extra subjects that they feel are important to the children.
   C. This can increase the educational motivation for the children.

III. Supporting paragraph 2: Topic sentence:

_____

_____

_____

A. Children who are gifted do not have to follow the pace of the others in the class.

B. _____

_____

IV. Supporting paragraph 3: Topic sentence: Finally, parents have the [3] excellent opportunity to spend quality time with their children [3].

A. _____

_____

B. _____

_____

V. Concluding paragraph (restates the thesis statement or gives an opinion or suggestion about the thesis statement)

PART B

The Writing Process: Practice Writing an Essay

Objectives

Prewriting:

Planning:

Partner feedback:

First draft:

Second Draft:
write a second draft

Editing:

  Grammar Focus:

  Sentence Check:

  Mechanics:

Final Draft:

In Part B, you will:

brainstorm ideas for an essay

write thesis, topic sentences, and supporting details in an outline

review classmates' outlines and analyze feedback

write an essay

use instructor or partner feedback to

verb tense review

adverb clauses

format of an essay

complete the final draft of the essay

The Writing Process: Writing Assignment

Your assignment is to write an original essay of five paragraphs explaining three categories of something. As you follow the steps in the writing process in this section, you will develop an outline for your essay, get partner feedback, and write the essay.

IMPORTANT NOTE:

You will study different kinds of essays in more detail in Blueprints 2

Prewriting: Brainstorming

Prewriting for an essay is no different from prewriting for a paragraph. You have practiced general brainstorming (Unit 1), freewriting (Unit 2), asking questions (Units 3 and 5), and making lists (Unit 4). Review these methods, and choose the one that works best for you. As you choose and narrow a topic, these guidelines may help you.

1. What subjects are you interested in (examples: sports, politics, movies, music)? Write a sample topic here:

   _____

   _____

2. Divide this topic into three types or categories (examples: folk music, classical music, rock music).

   _____

   _____

Sample Prewriting Activity

Joann decided that she wanted to write an essay about tennis. She used a cluster diagram as a prewriting technique.

TENNIS—Three categories

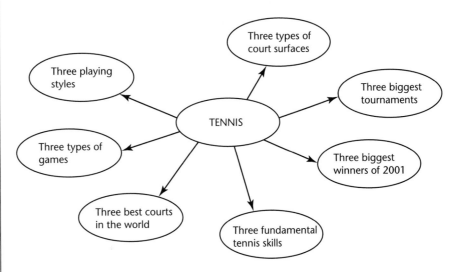

Planning: Write Thesis, Topic Sentences, and Supporting Details in an Outline

After thinking about all the categories, Joann decided to write an essay about three types of tennis surfaces: grass, clay, and asphalt. Here is her partial outline:

I. Introductory paragraph
  A. Hook (Give information about the standard size, equipment, and rules of tennis.)
  B. Narrowing information toward the thesis (Explain that there are some differences in tennis—the types of surfaces.)
  C. THESIS STATEMENT: The three most common types of tennis surfaces are grass, clay, and asphalt.

II. Supporting paragraph 1: Topic sentence: A grass surface tennis court is rare, but it is an excellent material to play on.
  A. Description of the surface
  B. How the surface affects the match (the ball, the players)

III. Supporting paragraph 2: Topic sentence: In addition to grass surface tennis courts, many tournaments are played on clay courts.
  A. Description of the surface
  B. How the surface affects the match (the ball, the players)

IV. Supporting paragraph 3: Topic sentence: The most commonly found type of tennis surface is asphalt.
  A. Description of the surface
  B. How the surface affects the match (the ball, the players)

V. Concluding paragraph (Restatement of thesis or opinion about which surface is preferable)

EXERCISE

5

WRITING OUTLINE NOTES

After you have decided on a topic and its three categories, follow these steps to write some outline notes. If you need help, review the example outlines on page 169.

1. Write your general topic in the box.

2. Develop a thesis statement that lists the three types or categories.

3. Write a topic sentence for one type or category next to each roman numeral.

4. In the spaces marked A, B, and C, write supporting details that explain your topic sentences.

5. Write a concluding idea that restates your thesis or gives your opinion.

TOPIC: _____

_____

THESIS STATEMENT:

_____

_____

_____

I. _____

    A. _____

    B. _____

    C. _____

II. _____

    A. _____

    B. _____

    C. _____

III. _____

    A. _____

    B. _____

    C. _____

CONCLUSION:

_____

_____

_____

EXERCISE

6

WRITING AN EXPANDED OUTLINE

Now expand your notes, and complete the outline below. Be sure to write a topic sentence for each supporting paragraph.

ESSAY OUTLINE

I. Introductory paragraph
   A. Hook
   B. Narrowing information toward the thesis
   C. THESIS STATEMENT:

   _____

   _____

   _____

II. Supporting paragraph 1: Topic sentence:

   _____

   _____

   A. _____

   _____

   B. _____

   _____

   C. _____

   _____

III. Supporting paragraph 2: Topic sentence:

   _____

   _____

   A. _____

   _____

   B. _____

   _____

   C. _____

   _____

IV. Supporting paragraph 3: Topic sentence:

_____

_____

A. _____

_____

B. _____

_____

C. _____

_____

V. Concluding paragraph (restates the thesis statement or gives an opinion or suggestion about the thesis statement)

_____

_____

Peer Review

Exchange outlines from Exercise 6 with another student. Read your partner's outline, and answer the questions on Partner Feedback Form: Unit 6, pp. 203–204. Discuss your partner's reactions to your outline. Make notes about any parts you need to change, and then revise your outline.

First Draft

You are now ready to write the first draft of your essay. Use your revised outline as a guide, and write five paragraphs about your topic. Then use this checklist to check your essay.

First Draft Checklist

1. Does my introductory paragraph contain a hook?

2. Does the thesis statement introduce three categories about my topic?

3. Is the number of categories in the thesis statement the same number of body paragraphs in my essay?

4. Check the topic sentence in each supporting paragraph. Does it talk about one category of my topic?

5. Did I write enough supporting details?

6. Did I use transition words correctly?

7. Does my concluding paragraph restate the thesis or give an opinion?

Editing: Grammar and Mechanics

Reviewing and practicing the following grammatical points will help you self-edit your essay for common grammatical mistakes.

Grammar Focus: Verb Tense Review

The three main verb tenses are the present, the past, and the future. Within these tenses are several different options.

❶ PRESENT TENSE

A. The simple present is used for things that are generally known to be true.

Examples:

Water *boils* at 212 degrees Fahrenheit.

The planets *rotate* around the sun.

The simple present can also be used for events that are true now.

Examples:

Harold *works* at IBM.

My mother and father *are* on vacation.

IMPORTANT NOTE:

An important rule to remember for the simple present is that the third person singular takes an *-s* when the verb is regular.

Examples:

Greta *sings*.

He *studies*.

She *dances*.

B. The present progressive, which is also called the present continuous, takes the form (*am / is / are*) + *VERB* + *ing*. It is used to describe what is happening at this moment.

Examples:

Brittany and Lisa *are watching* TV.

The dogs *are barking* and *waking* up all the neighbors.

The present continuous can also describe an action that will occur in the immediate future. In this usage, the actual time is usually stated directly (see the underlined parts of the examples).

Examples:

I *am going* to the mall <u>this afternoon</u>.

The members of the European Community *are meeting* in the Hague <u>in a few weeks</u>.

❷ PRESENT PERFECT TENSE

The present perfect tense shows action that began in the past and continues in the present or may be completed in the present. The present perfect takes the form *have/has + past participle of the main verb.*

Because of its many uses, the present perfect can fall into three general categories: indefinite past tense, repeated past tense action, and continuation of an action from the past to now. Note that some present perfect actions are actually in the past and some are continuing now.

Examples:

A. Indefinite past tense:

Brianna *has seen* that movie. (She saw that movie at some unspecified time in the past.)

B. Repeated past tense action:

The Brazilian National Soccer Team *has won* the World Cup at least four times. (The action was repeated in the past.)

C. Continuation of an action from the past to now:

The French language students *have studied* together since January. (They began to study in the past and continue in the present. This form is usually expressed with *since* and *for*. Common verbs for this usage are *live, study, work,* and *wear*.)

❸ PAST TENSE

A. The past tense describes actions that happened in the past. The simple past refers to an action that is finished. It began and ended in the past.

Examples:

John F. Kennedy *died* in 1963.

I *finished* the book last night.

Many verbs in English are irregular, and you need to study their forms.

Examples:

Justin *went* to the baseball game last week. (past of *go*)

We *saw* that movie three days ago. (past of *see*)

B. The past tense can also take the progressive form of *was / were + VERB + ing.*

This tense is commonly used for an action that was happening at a specific time in the past.

Examples:

Last night at 7:30, I *was eating* dinner with my family.

The past progressive can also explain an action that was interrupted by something (usually another action.) The interruption often includes the word *when.*

Examples:

We *were studying* in the library when the fire alarm went off.

When you refer to two things that occurred at the same time, use *while* with the first action and put both verbs in the past progressive.

Examples:

While the instructor *was grading* the essays, the students *were taking* a grammar test.

❹ FUTURE TENSE

Form the simple future most often by using the modal verb *will + VERB*.

Examples:

The congressional leaders *will meet* in the near future to discuss the proposed bill.

Another way of forming the simple future tense is to use *be going to + VERB*.

Examples:

The congressional leaders *are going to meet* in the near future to discuss the proposed bill.

EXERCISE

7

WORKING WITH VERB TENSES

Read the following sentences. In the blanks, write the correct form of the verb in parentheses ( ).

1. The nursing students (receive) _____ their exam grades yesterday, but most of them (be, not) _____ happy when the tests were returned.

2. They (study) _____ Physical Anatomy at the library right now, but they (return) _____ home by 9:00 P.M.

3. The student nurses (be) _____ in the program only two semesters, and they (graduate) _____ in one and a half years.

4. That *Gray's Anatomy* book (belong) _____ to Michael, and he wants it back.

5. Don't bother Susan right now. She (learn) _____ to draw blood from a patient.

6. Dr. Iverson (teach) _____ in the LPN program for ten years, and he (want) _____ to continue for at least another ten years.

7. Yesterday, while some of the student nurses (practice) _____ blood pressure techniques, others (evaluate) _____ pulse rates.

8. The nurse practitioner (give) _____ a lecture on medical ethics when I walked into the classroom.

Sentence Check: Adverb Clauses

Like adverbs, adverb clauses usually tell *why, how, when, where,* or *with what result* about the verb. Adverb clauses always begin with connecting words called subordinating conjunctions (SC).

SC   Adverb clause

Example: **If the weather is nice**, we'll play golf tomorrow.

Here is a list of common subordinating conjunctions used in adverb clauses.

Cause/effect:	as, because, since, so that, that
Concession:	although, as if even if, even though, though
Condition:	if, if only, since, unless, when, whenever, whether
Compare/contrast:	as, as if, as though, whereas, while, whether
Purpose:	in order that, so that
Space or time:	after, as long as, before, once, since, until, when, whenever

Examples:

<u>Because it is raining</u>, the picnic has been postponed. (tells *why*)

The picnic has been postponed <u>because it is raining</u>.

<u>After he finishes the reading</u>, the author will sign autographs. (tells *when*)

The author will sign autographs <u>after he finishes the reading</u>.

<u>If more homes are sold</u>, the new housing development can make a profit. (tells *how* or *with what result*)

The new housing development can make a profit <u>if more homes are sold.</u>

IMPORTANT NOTE:

When you begin a sentence with an adverb clause, put a comma after it. If you put the adverb clause at the end of the sentence, usually no comma is needed.

EXERCISE

8

ADDING TO ADVERB CLAUSES

Read the following sentences. Then make up an independent clause to make a complete sentence. Add commas where necessary.

1. If you know the answer to the question _____

   _____ .

2. Before Lisa came to school _____

   _____ .

3. _____

   _____ although he had a free ticket.

4. Whenever I take my puppy out for a walk _____

   _____ .

5. _____

   _____

   so that you will have some room in your stomach for dessert.

6. If a business wants to succeed globally _____

   _____ .

7. Before the company decided to launch its new product in China

   _____

   _____ .

8. _____

_____

although the marketing research was recent.

9. Whenever a new product is introduced in another country

_____

_____ .

10. _____

_____

so that the customers will know what to expect from this new product.

WRITING ADVERB CLAUSES

Read the following sentences and fill in the missing adverb clause. Use the subordinating conjunctions in parentheses. Add commas where necessary.

1. (if) _____

I will move to California.

2. (before) The twins studied medicine _____

_____ .

3. (although) _____

he got the highest grade on the exam.

4. (whenever) _____

I buy postage stamps.

5. (so that) Raul is saving extra money _____

_____ .

6. (if) _____

James will become a nurse practitioner.

7. (after) The twins were born _____

_____ .

8. (although) _____

the new French perfume didn't sell very well in the United States.

9. (whenever) _____

people tend to go out and taste this new ice cream flavor.

10. (so that) Rebekah is studying in a nursing program _____

_____ .

FINDING ADVERB CLAUSES

Reread "Global Marketing Strategies" on pages 154–155 and "Nursing Choices" on pages 161–162. Then work with a partner, and in each essay, underline the adverb clauses and circle the subordinating conjunctions.

Mechanics: Essay Format

In your college work, most essays follow a similar format. Your instructor may give you a specific essay format for a particular course, but the format below is the standard one that you can use in most cases. As you study it, keep these things in mind:

▶ Use 12-point type.

▶ Leave 1-inch margins on all sides.

▶ Indent each paragraph using five spaces, or use the tab feature.

▶ Do not underline or bold your title.

▶ Be sure your name appears on every page.

[1 inch margin]

Your name

Professor's name

Title of course

Date

Essay Title

Paragraph 1 (indented)

Paragraph 2 (indented)

_____ [new page] _____

Your last name and page number

Paragraph 3 (indented)

Paragraph 4 (indented)

_____ [new page] _____

Your last name and page number

Paragraph 5 (indented)

[1 inch margin]

Write Your Second Draft

As you write a second draft of your essay, use the format you just studied. Then check the following items. Make corrections where necessary.

Second Draft Checklist

1. Do you have past tense in your essay? Most essays that deal with types of existing things (kinds of cars, types of personalities, methods of transportation) are written in the present tense. If you have past tense, do you have a clear reason to use the past tense in those examples?

2. How many adverb clauses do you have? _____ Does each adverb clause have a subject and a verb? _____

3. Did you include a title for your essay? If not, add one now.

4. Look at the Partner Feedback Form that you used for your outline. Is all the information included in your essay? It can help you check to make sure your essay is complete.

Final Draft

Carefully revise your essay, using all of the feedback you have received: partner feedback, instructor comments, and self-evaluation. In addition, try reading your essay aloud. This can help you find awkward-sounding sentences and errors in punctuation. When you have finished, neatly type your final draft using the format on page 180.

Additional Writing Assignments from the Academic Disciplines

Beginning with the prewriting activity on page 169, go through the writing process and write another five-paragraph essay. Choose a topic from the following list.

SUBJECT	*WRITING TASK*
Technology	Explain three types of Internet connections that are currently available.
Science	Choose three methods of obtaining energy. Explain these three methods.
The arts	Think about painting styles. Classify them into three main groups.
Management	Consider management techniques. Write an essay describing three specific types.
Practical	Write an essay about three ways of studying effectively for an exam.

Documenting Information from Sources

When you include information from an original source in the final draft of your paragraphs or essays, you must cite this source. There are several styles of citing material. One of the most common ones is to list the author of the material and the publication date.

In the examples that follow, note how the student writer uses part of Zumdahl's information in his work. Pay attention to the wording of the original source, the wording of the student writing, and the manner in which the information is cited.

ORIGINAL SOURCE

Although some chemical industries have been culprits in the past for fouling the earth's environment, that situation is rapidly changing. In fact, a quiet revolution is sweeping through chemistry from academic labs to Fortune 500 companies. Chemistry is going green. *Green chemistry* means minimizing hazardous wastes, substituting water and other environmentally friendlier substances for traditional organic solvents, and manufacturing productions out of recyclable materials.

From *Introductory Chemistry* by Steven Zumdahl. Copyright © 2000 Houghton Mifflin Company. Reprinted with permission.

Possible citation: According to Zumdahl (2000), green chemistry has three basic components.

Possible citation: Zumdahl (2000) discusses the quiet revolution that is taking place within the chemistry world.

STUDENT WRITING USING THE ORIGINAL SOURCE

Most people would regard chemistry as a very traditional branch of science, but there are new hybrids of this traditional science. Green chemistry is a good example of a new version of a traditional field of study. *According to Zumdahl (2000), green chemistry has three basic components, including creating fewer dangerous wastes, using water as a solvent, and creating products from recycled materials.* Because it is so new, green chemistry has yet to prove itself to be a true advancement over traditional chemistry. However, green chemistry seems to have a great deal of potential.

Common ways for writing the citation include the following:

- ► *According to* Giblin, this medicine has serious problems . . .
- ► Giblin *found* that this medicine had serious problems . . .
- ► Giblin *reported* that this medicine had serious problems . . .
- ► A report by Giblin *showed* that this medicine had serious problems . . .
- ► Giblin *concluded* that this medicine had serious problems . . .
- ► *On the basis of* Giblin's findings, we may conclude that . . .
- ► *On the basis of* Giblin's results, it may be concluded that . . .
- ► *Because of* Giblin's results, this medicine is no longer used . . .
- ► *From* Giblin's work, we know that this medicine has serious problems . . .
- ► Giblin *proved* that this medicine has serious problems . . .

IMPORTANT NOTE:

If your field has a special guide for citations, follow the rules or guidelines in that booklet. Examples of special guides for citations include MLA (Modern Language Association), APA (American Psychological Association), and *The Chicago Manual of Style* published by the University of Chicago).

Run-On Sentences

A **run-on** sentence is a combination of two (or more) sentences that are written together without any punctuation between them.

Run-on: The giraffe is native to parts of Africa this animal has several ways of protecting itself.

Run-on: The main airline serving Memphis is Northwest other airlines serving this city include Delta and American.

One easy way to correct a run-on error is to write two separate sentences that begin with capital letters and end with correct final punctuation.

Correct: The giraffe is native to parts of Africa. This animal has several ways of protecting itself.

Correct: The main airline serving Memphis is Northwest. Other airlines serving this city include Delta and American.

Another way to correct a run-on is to connect the two separate sentences with a semicolon (;).

Correct: The giraffe is native to parts of Africa; this animal has several ways of protecting itself.

Correct: The main airline serving Memphis is Northwest; other airlines serving this city include Delta and American.

Another way to correct a run-on sentence is to add a connecting word. The connecting word will depend on the relationship between the information in the two sentences.

Correct: The main airline serving Memphis is Northwest, but other airlines serving this city include Delta and American.

Another way to correct a run-on sentence is to put the information in one part of the sentence into a dependent clause.

Correct: The giraffe, which is native to parts of Africa, has several ways of protecting itself.

EXERCISE

1

IDENTIFYING RUN-ON SENTENCES

Identify each sentence as correct (C) or run-on (RO). If the sentence is a run-on, make a correction.

_____ 1. The weather in January is usually cold and damp. The weather

in October is usually cool and dry.

_____ 2. Most of the voters said that they voted for Williams a small percentage indicated that they voted for his opponent.

_____ 3. The largest countries in South America are Brazil and Argentina, and the largest countries in North America are Canada and the United States.

_____ 4. People react differently to different colors yellow seems to cheer people up while blue makes people sad.

_____ 5. To pass the driver's license exam, you must get at least 60% in each of the two parts of the test.

_____ 6. The time that the artist spent in Europe helped him later on with his European paintings.

_____ 7. The terms for keeping score in tennis are a bit odd. For example, deuce and love-thirty make tennis novices nervous.

_____ 8. Julia Roberts has two new movies this year. Movie critics have indicated that they have not reached a consensus regarding the quality of either of these movies.

EXERCISE 2

CORRECTING RUN-ON SENTENCES

Rewrite the following paragraphs. Correct the three run-on sentences.

A business firm controls four important elements of marketing it combines them in a way that reaches the firm's target market. These are the _product_ itself, the _price_ of the product, the means chosen for its _distribution,_ and the _promotion_ of the product when combined, these four elements form a marketing mix.

A firm can vary its marketing mix by changing any one or more of these ingredients. Thus, a firm may use one marketing mix to reach one target market and a second, somewhat different marketing mix to reach another target market. For example, most auto makers produce several different types and models of vehicles they aim these different types at different market segments based on age, income, and other factors.

From _Business,_ Sixth Edition, by Pride, Hughes, & Kapoor. Copyright © 1999
Houghton Mifflin Company. Reprinted with permission.

Comma Splices

A **comma splice** is a run-on sentence that is a combination of two (or more) sentences that are written together with only a comma between them.

Comma splice: The giraffe is native to parts of Africa, this animal has several ways of protecting itself.

Comma splice: The main airline serving Memphis is Northwest, other airlines serving this city include Delta and American.

One easy way to correct a comma splice is to write two separate sentences that begin with capital letters and end with correct final punctuation.

Correct: The giraffe is native to parts of Africa. This animal has several ways of protecting itself.

Correct: The main airline serving Memphis is Northwest. Other airlines serving this city include Delta and American.

Another way is to connect the two separate sentences with a semicolon (;).

Correct: The giraffe is native to parts of Africa; this animal has several ways of protecting itself.

Correct: The main airline serving Memphis is Northwest; other airlines serving this city include Delta and American.

Another way to correct a comma splice is to add a connecting word. The connecting word will depend on the relationship between the information in the two sentences.

Correct: The main airline serving Memphis is Northwest, but other airlines serving this city include Delta and American.

Another way to correct a comma splice is to put the information in one part of the sentence into a dependent clause.

Correct: The giraffe, which is native to parts of Africa, has several ways of protecting itself.

EXERCISE

1

IDENTIFYING COMMA SPLICE SENTENCES

Identify each sentence as correct (C) or comma splice (CS). If the sentence is a comma splice, make a correction.

_____ 1. The weather in January is usually cold and damp, the weather in

October is usually cool and dry.

_____ 2. Most of the voters said that they voted for Williams, a small percentage indicated that they voted for his opponent.

_____ 3. The largest countries in South America are Brazil and Argentina, and the largest countries in North America are Canada and the United States.

_____ 4. People react differently to different colors. Yellow seems to cheer people up while blue makes people sad.

_____ 5. To pass the driver's license exam, you must get at least 60% in each of the two parts of the test.

_____ 6. The time that the artist spent in Europe helped him later on with his European paintings.

_____ 7. The terms for keeping score in tennis are a bit odd, for example, deuce and love-thirty make tennis novices nervous.

_____ 8. Julia Roberts has two new movies this year, movie critics have indicated that they have not reached a consensus regarding the quality of either of these movies.

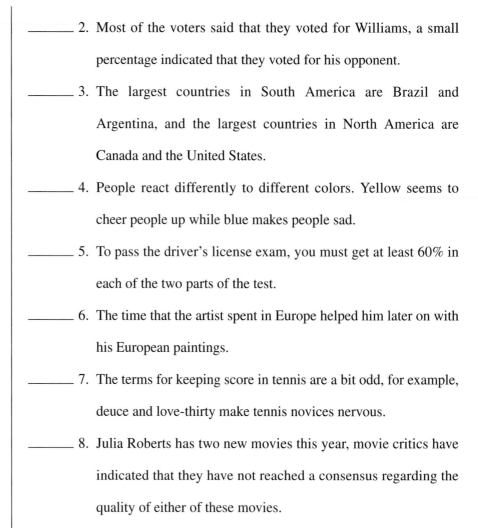

EXERCISE

2

CORRECTING COMMA SPLICE SENTENCES

Rewrite the following paragraphs. Correct the two comma splice sentences.

A business firm controls four important elements of marketing, it combines them in a way that reaches the firm's target market. These are the _product_ itself, the _price_ of the product, the means chosen for its _distribution_, and the _promotion_ of the product. When combined, these four elements form a marketing mix.

A firm can vary its marketing mix by changing any one or more of these ingredients. Thus, a firm may use one marketing mix to reach one target market and a second, somewhat different marketing mix to reach another target market, for example, most auto makers produce several different types and models of vehicles. They aim these different types at different market segments based on age, income, and other factors.

From _Business,_ Sixth Edition, by Pride, Hughes, & Kapoor. Copyright © 1999 Houghton Mifflin Company. Reprinted with permission.

Fragments

A **fragment** is an incomplete sentence. A fragment usually contains a verb or a subject, but there is not a complete subject-verb arrangement.

Fragment: Has several ways of protecting itself.

Fragment: The main airline serving Memphis Northwest.

One easy way to correct a fragment is to add the missing subject or the missing verb.

Correct: This animal has several ways of protecting itself.

Correct: The main airline serving Memphis is Northwest.

Another way to correct a fragment is to connect it to the sentence it goes with.

Incorrect: Some birds return to the same nests each year. For example, the osprey.

Correct: Some birds return to the same nests each year, for example, the osprey.

EXERCISE

1

IDENTIFYING FRAGMENTS

Identify each sentence as correct (C) or fragment (F). If the sentence is a fragment, make a correction.

_____ 1. The weather in October is usually cool and dry.

_____ 2. A small percentage of the people that voted for Kennedy.

_____ 3. The largest countries in South America are Brazil and Argentina, and the largest countries in North America Canada and the United States.

_____ 4. Yellow seems to cheer people up while blue makes people sad.

_____ 5. To pass the driver's license exam, must get at least 60 percent in each of the two parts of the test.

_____ 6. The time that the artist spent in Europe.

_____ 7. The terms for keeping score in tennis are a bit odd. For example, deuce and love-thirty.

_____ 8. Julia Roberts has two new movies this year. Movie critics have indicated that they have not reached a consensus regarding the quality of either of these movies.

EXERCISE

2

CORRECTING FRAGMENTS

Rewrite the following paragraphs. There are four fragments. Be sure to identify these errors and correct them.

A business firm controls four important elements of marketing. Combines them in a way that reaches the firm's target market. These are the *product* itself, the *price* of the product, the means chosen for its *distribution*, and the *promotion* of the product. When combined. These four elements form a marketing mix.

A firm can vary its marketing mix. By changing any one or more of these ingredients. Thus, may use one marketing mix to reach one target market and a second, somewhat different marketing mix to reach another target market. For example, most auto makers produce several different types and models of vehicles. They aim these different types at different market segments based on age, income, and other factors.

From *Business,* Sixth Edition, by Pride, Hughes, & Kapoor. Copyright © 1999
Houghton Mifflin Company. Reprinted with permission.

_____

_____

_____

_____

_____

_____

_____

_____

_____

Partner Feedback Forms

Partner Feedback Form:
Unit 1   The Paragraph

Writer: _____ Partner Reviewer: _____

Date: _____

1. In one or two words, what is the topic of the paragraph?

   _____

2. What is the controlling idea? _____

3. How many sentences are there? _____ Does each sentence begin with a capital letter? _____ Does each sentence end with a punctuation mark? _____

4. Can you find a topic sentence? _____ If so, write it here: _____

5. Write one supporting sentence here. _____ Does this sentence relate to the topic sentence? _____ If not, suggest how it could be revised. _____

6. Can you find a concluding sentence? _____ If so, write it here: _____

7. Do the topic sentence and the concluding sentence contain similar information? _____ Do you think that these two sentences work well together in this paragraph? _____

8. Look for the transitions *in addition (to), though* and *although,* and *later* in the paragraph. Did the writer use any? _____ If so, write them here. _____

9. Were any parts of the paragraph not clear to you? _____ If so, circle those parts on your partner's paper.

10. Is there any information that you think is missing from the paragraph? If so, what? _____

Peer Feedback Form:
Unit 2 Descriptive Paragraphs

Writer: _____ Partner Reviewer: _____

Date: _____

1. In one or two words, what is the topic of the paragraph?

   _____

2. Can you find a topic sentence? _____ If so, write it

   here: _____

3. Can you find a concluding sentence? _____ If so,

   write it here: _____

4. Circle all the descriptive words and phrases you can find.

5. Is there enough description? _____ If not, can you

   think of how to add more description to make the paragraph seem

   more vivid? Suggest some descriptive words and phrases here.

   _____

6. Does the paragraph follow a logical organization using either time or

   space? _____ Which kind of organization is used?

   _____

7. Do the transition words help the paragraph flow from one idea to

   another? _____ Look for *when, as, while,* and *after*

   as well as *in addition (to), though* and *although,* and *later.* Make any

   suggestions for improvement here. _____

8. Were there any parts of the paragraph that were not clear to you?

   _____ If so, circle those parts on your partner's

   paper.

9. Is there any information that you think is missing from the

   paragraph? _____ If so, what?_____

Partner Feedback Form:
Unit 3　Process Paragraphs

Writer: _____ Partner Reviewer: _____

Date: _____

1. In one or two words, what is the topic of the paragraph?

   _____

2. Does the paragraph have a title? _____ If not,

   suggest a title here: _____

3. How many steps does the writer include in the process described in

   this paragraph? _____

4. In your own words, write the final step in the process.

   _____

5. Does the writer use the transition words *first, next, then,* and *finally*

   to put the steps in chronological order? _____ If not,

   make corrections on the paper.

6. Underline any compound sentences and circle the conjunction used.

   Is it the correct conjunction? _____ If not, make

   corrections on the paper.

7. Were there any parts of the paragraph that were not clear to you?

   _____ If so, circle those parts on your partner's

   paper. Write a question here about one of the circled parts. What do

   you want to ask the writer? _____

8. Is there any information that you think is missing from the

   paragraph? _____ If so, what? _____

   _____

Partner Feedback Form:
Unit 4 Definition Paragraphs

Writer: _____ Partner Reviewer: _____

Date: _____

1. Does the paragraph have a title? _____ If not,

   suggest a title here: _____

2. What word or term is being defined? _____

3. Is there a clear definition sentence for the term? _____

   If yes, write it here. (If not, write a good definition sentence here.)

   _____

   _____

4. Did you know the meaning of this term before you read this

   paragraph? _____ If not, did the information in the

   paragraph and the way it was written help you to understand the

   meaning? _____ Write additional comments on your

   answer here: _____

   _____

5. Did the writer include any examples in the definition paragraph?

   _____ If so, how many? _____ List

   one of them here. _____ If not, suggest an example

   here. _____ Put the letters (EX) with a

   circle around them in the paragraph where your suggested example

   could be placed.

6. Can you find any adjective clauses in the paragraph?

   _____ If so, write one here. _____

   _____

   If not, underline two shorter sentences that could be combined into a longer sentence with an adjective clause. Then write your newly

created sentence with adjective clause here. _____

_____

7. Were there any parts of the paragraph that were not clear to you?

_____ If so, circle those parts on your partner's paper.

8. Is there any information that you think is missing from the

paragraph? _____ If so, what? _____

_____

Partner Feedback Form: Unit 5 Comparison/Contrast Paragraphs

Writer: _____ Partner Reviewer: _____

Date: _____

1. In one or two words, what is the topic of the paragraph?

   _____

2. Does the paragraph have a title? _____ If not,

   suggest a title here: _____

3. How many sentences are there? _____

4. Can you find a topic sentence? _____ If so, write it

   here: _____

   _____

5. Write the two main ideas that are being compared:

   _____

   _____

6. List two ways in which these ideas are similar.

   a. _____

   b. _____

7. List two ways in which these ideas are different.

   a. _____

   b. _____

8. Does the writer use the transition words *like, the same . . . as, in*

   contrast, and *whereas* to signal a shift in thinking? _____

   Note any corrections needed on your partner's paper.

9. Does the concluding sentence mention both topics? _____

   If not, suggest a revision here:

   _____

   _____

10. Were any parts of the paragraph not clear to you? _____

    Circle them and ask the writer to clarify them for you. Write the

    clarification here. _____

11. Is there any information that you think is missing from the

    paragraph? If so, what? _____

    _____

    _____

Partner Feedback Form:
Unit 6 Introducing the Essay

Writer: _____ Partner Reviewer: _____

Date: _____

1. In one or two words, what is the topic of the essay?

   _____

2. Does the outline have a thesis statement? _____ If

   not, write a sample thesis statement. _____

   _____

3. What are the three categories that will be explained in the essay?

   _____

   _____

4. Does the writer use the transition words *for example, for instance,*

   one . . . , another . . . , or *such as* correctly in the topic sentences for

   the supporting paragraphs? _____ If not, suggest

   corrections here. _____

   _____

5. In the supporting section, are there any details listed that you think

   do not relate to the topic of the paragraph? _____ If so,

   write them here. _____

   _____

6. Does the conclusion information sound like a logical ending to this

   essay? _____ What does the conclusion here do:

   Make a suggestion? Offer an opinion? Make a prediction?

   _____ If not, can you make a suggestion for ending

   the essay? _____

   _____

7. Was there any part of the organization of the outline that was not

   clear to you? _____ Circle those parts.

8. Is there any information that you think is missing from the outline?

   _____ If so, what? _____

   _____